Everyday Psalms

. . . The Power of the Psalms
in language and images
for today

James Taylor

WOOD LAKE BOOKS

Editing: Jim Taylor, Mike Schwartzentruber
Cover design: Margaret Kyle
Cover photo: www.photos.com

We acknowledge the financial support of the Government of Canada through the Book
Publishing Industry Development Program for our publishing activities.

At Wood Lake Books we practice what we publish, guided by a concern for fairness,
justice, and equal opportunity in all of our relationships with employees and customers.

Wood Lake Books Inc. is committed to caring for the environment and all creation. We
recycle, reuse and compost, and encourage readers to do the same. Resources are printed
on recycled paper and more environmentally friendly groundwood papers (newsprint),
whenever possible. A portion of all profit is donated to charitable organizations.

Note:
The psalm paraphrases in this book may be reproduced as bulletin inserts provided
that credit is given to the author and publisher. In all other instances, full copyright
restrictions, as specified below, apply.

Canadian Cataloguing in Publication Data
Taylor, James, 1936–
Everyday Psalms
Includes index.
ISBN 1–55145–045–3
1. Bible. O.T. Psalms—Paraphrases, English.
I. Title.
BS1440.T39 1994   223'.205209   C94–910602–x

Published by
Wood Lake Books Inc.
Kelowna, British Columbia, Canada
www.woodlakebooks.com

Printing 10 9 8 7 6 5

Printed in Canada by
Blitz Print

TABLE OF CONTENTS

PREFACE

When I was young, I had to memorize some of the psalms. At the time, I hated it. I considered it punishment. Since then, I have been grateful, for those historic words have given me comfort and insight time after time.

Over hundreds of years, for many thousands of people, the psalms have been a source of strength and comfort. But I deliberately make that statement in the past tense. They **have been**... I am not convinced that they are any more.

Things have changed too much. The world is dramatically different. Simply shifting archaic language into modern words doesn't make the old psalms meaningful.

Changing metaphors and images

The problem lies not in the words as much as in the images and metaphors. In our time, educated by a commitment to democracy and a rejection of the Vietnam war, we no longer think in ancient pictures of kings and shepherds, battles and armies, opponents and victors.

The dominant image for our time, I suspect, is "family." When we want to express values of love, respect, caring, loyalty, faithfulness, dependability, responsibility, even discipline—for all these, we tend to find examples from within the family.

But the original psalms hardly mention family—certainly not in the sense we understand it. The only exception I recall comes in Psalm 103: "as a father pitieth his children..." By contrast, there are dozens upon dozens of military images, expecting God to be revealed in conquest and victory.

We don't have many kings around any more, and those we do have don't dare act like biblical rulers. Few of us—even in farming communities—encounter shepherds regularly. Yet for about half of the psalms, the dominant metaphor is shepherd/king.

In our world, we are much more likely to deal with automatic transmissions and broken families, with mortgages and psychoses, with operating rooms and refugees. The **message** hasn't necessarily changed; the **metaphor used to express it** has.

If the psalms are to continue to have value to contemporary readers, we need to update the images, not just the words.

Every age and culture chooses its own metaphors for its ideals. When the writers of the original psalms wanted to provide a concrete image of fairness, or of loyalty, or of compassion, they would choose an idealized king, one like David, perhaps. That metaphor worked in a fairly small, close-knit, nation which saw the king as the representative of the total community. It does not work today. Even a deeply respected ruler like Queen Elizabeth doesn't have the kind of personal relationship with her subjects that David had with his—let alone the power to arbitrarily intervene. And given our chronic antipathy to all governments and leaders, we could not simply substitute the name of a current Prime Minister or President. That would make a mockery out of the message of the psalm.

Not only are some of the images in the psalms outdated, they're offensive. We have moved beyond slavery, for example. We reject genocide. Some of the psalms advocate a level of violence, of vengeance upon one's enemies, that we would no longer consider acceptable—though we might secretly wish it. Some of the psalms treat God as a kind of house god of the Israelites. Other religions of the region had their house gods, their private deities. So the psalms sometimes imply that God belonged exclusively to the Hebrew people, with no concern for anyone else.

We have, I think, outgrown most of those concepts. We have, I hope, learned something since then. Between the time when the psalms were written down and now, we have been exposed to the lives and teachings of both Jesus and the great Hebrew prophets. The prophets dramatically expanded Israel's vision of the nature of God. Jesus **showed** us the nature of God. Leaders of the early church, like Paul, amplified and interpreted that knowledge for us.

The only way to make the psalms relevant for our time, I concluded, was to find new images entirely. And where I could, without doing violence to the content of the psalms themselves, I have incorporated some newer and fuller understandings of God's nature and intent for us.

What I've tried to do, in effect, is to present the psalms as the original psalmists might have written them, if they were living in our time.

Everyday psalms

I see three profound reasons why I—or anyone else—can and should amend the psalms.

1. The psalms themselves make no pretence of being divine dictation. The psalms were written by, and for, the Hebrew people themselves. Very often, the psalm is credited to a specific individual: for example, David or Asaph.

The psalms were Hebrew hymns. As hymns, they are no more sacred than the words of Samuel Wesley or Frederick Kaan. Our hymns are interpretations of divine wisdom; so were the psalms. When our churches publish a revised hymn book, we do not reject the old hymns—we provide words and music that can better speak to the needs of a new audience. New paraphrases of the psalms perform the same function.

2. The psalms were about the present-day experience of their people. They didn't deal with hypothetical situations or, in the main, with history. They dealt with real life.

The writers of the psalms were, at times, brutally honest about their feelings. They pulled no punches. About a third of the psalms are bitter laments, collective or personal. If they felt God had betrayed them, they said so. If they felt like a worm, they said so. If they wanted their enemies' faces rubbed in the dirt, they said so.

We, in our time, are likely to feel that we have to be careful about the words we use in speaking to God. We must not complain, because God knows best; we must not be crude, or flippant, any more than we would be with a judge or a prime minister; we don't want to sound too gushy, because flattery is impolite. The writers of the psalms suffered from no such inhibitions.

3.   We have the example of Jesus. To a people accustomed to telling their story by saying, "Once we were slaves in Egypt..." Jesus told present-day parables. He told about people getting mugged and robbed on a journey, about merchants buying and selling, about losing and finding something valuable, about bread and wine and seeds and yeast. Commonplace, ordinary, everyday things. So our psalms need to be about everyday things too.

None of this denies the validity of the Bible, or seeks to replace it—any more than Jesus' message denied or replaced the Hebrew scriptures, the only Bible he knew. It simply provides alternative images. My paraphrases need to be read in tandem with the historic versions. I hope and believe that they will offer new insights into familiar phrases, making the originals even more meaningful.

Key characteristics

For people of my age, the most familiar versions of the psalms come from the King James Version of the Bible. They, in turn, borrowed heavily from William Tyndale's inspired translations. They set the standard for what psalms should be, in English.

Many contemporary paraphrases, in my view, turn the historic psalms into blah. They replace the vivid and concrete images (for their time) with generalized abstractions.

In these paraphrases, I have tried to retain some of the key characteristics that make the psalms of the King James Version so memorable.

1.   The psalms are **poetry**. Poetry depends on its wealth of images and metaphors. Poems are not analytic reports or recipes. Their figures of speech fall all over each other. In the overlapping of these images and analogies, the message comes through.

2.   The psalms are **Hebrew** poetry. The Hebrews did not use rhymes and formal rhythms the way we do. Their poetry took a different form. Typically, it balanced two or more meanings, the way children balance on a teeter-totter. The second, third, or even fourth parts might complement the opening part with a matching restatement, or supplement it with more information, or negate it by stating the opposite.

Because it was oral (antiphonal) poetry, various readers or

groups tossed these balancing phrases back and forth, rather like a ping-pong ball flying back and forth across the table—sometimes the volley lasted only a few strokes, and sometimes it went on and on.

That is why we, in our churches, developed responsive readings of psalms. We usually divide the parts verse by verse; in fact, the division is often within verses. In my paraphrases, I've tried to show the balancing elements by using boldface text.

They also used alliteration and assonance to link the balanced parts. Instead of rhyme, Hebrew poetry used sound. Each side of the equation incorporated certain sounds, as well as certain meanings. The writers of the King James Version accomplished this technique brilliantly—it may be the only time in history that a committee produced great literature! I have tried to do it, wherever I could, without being artificial.

I admit that I have taken certain liberties. The psalms are sometimes disjointed. They weren't always written as one coherent piece. Over time, bits and pieces of songs have sometimes gotten glued together. For the sake of clarity, I have occasionally taken verses out of order; at other times, I have ignored verses that, for one reason or another, just didn't seem to fit.

Using these psalms

In reading these psalms, or using them liturgically in worship services, you should take the same liberties. If the psalm paraphrase is too long, use only part of it. If something doesn't work, leave it out. If you can improve on the antiphonal readings I have suggested, do it. If I've written it as first person singular "I," and you prefer first person plural "we," perhaps for liturgical use in a worship service, and if it will work, go ahead and make the changes. Change the pronouns from feminine to masculine, or vice versa, if the paraphrase will mean more to you that way.

If these paraphrases stimulate you to go back to the historic versions, and to rewrite or retell them out of your own experience—or even to write your own new psalms based on your own life and learning—my efforts will be richly repaid.

—Jim Taylor

PSALM 1
Rooted in righteousness

1   Happy are those who refuse to be led astray.

The lure of selfish living whispers in my ears.
Opportunities to profit from another's pain
constantly cross my path.
Even if I avoid those traps,
the temptation to scorn others taunts me.

2   Happy are those
who keep their eyes on the distant vision
of how God intended life to be lived,
who think on that vision, every step of the way.

3   They stand like trees growing by a lake.
Their roots go down deep,
drawing strength from the whole history of human experience,
waters that will never dry up.
They blossom in spring and bear fruit in the fall.
They will not wither in tough times.

4   **The drifters are not like that;**
their roots are as shallow as tumbleweed.
In the heat of summer, they blow away in the wind.
They have nothing to hold them upright.
They cannot hold on when storms howl.
5   They are neither gathered like hay nor picked like apples.
They have no worth or value;
Their influence will not last long among us.

6   **God knows who is in the right;**
We will see whose work survives when winter comes.

        James Taylor

PSALM 1
The source of happiness

1 Happiness can't be captured.
Like a wild bird or a bouncing ball,
it is always just beyond your grasp.
It is not found in fads or fashions,
nor in climbing to the top of the heap.
2 Happiness comes from immersing yourself in God.
Instead of struggling to stay on top,
yield yourself to the deep flow of God's universe.
3 You will not drown.
You will be swept along by forces beyond your imagining.

4, 5 Foam on the surface blows about;
driftwood piles up on sandbars;
people obsessed with themselves
end up as rotting debris on the rocks.
But the current rolls on.

6 To find happiness, let yourself be carried away
by something stronger than a social eddy.

PSALM 2:1–6, 10–12
Privilege and power

The second half of Psalm 1. Psalm 1 is about the righteous;
Psalm 2 describes the fate of the unrighteous.

1 Why do powerful people huddle together,
hatching their self-serving policies?
2 **They assume that they were chosen to rule.**
They put their heads together
to keep themselves in power.
3 **They tell themselves:**
"I refuse to be restricted;
I must have freedom to act as I see fit."

4	**God laughs at them;**
5	**God will brush them off like dandruff;**
	they will cower in fear.
6	**God says: "I choose my own representatives;**
	I have no contract with you."

10	**Smarten up, you executives.**
	Wise up, you governments.
11	**God has a quick temper.**
	Serve the Lord, not yourselves;
	Or God will be angry,
12a	**and flick you into eternity.**

PSALM 2
The mighty will fall

1	What causes powerful people to plot together
	for their own profit?
2	**They manipulate events to preserve their privileges.**
3	They try to take matters into their own hands;
	they think they are greater than God.
4	But God laughs at their vanity.
5	**They will see how fast their success fades.**
	Their foundations will crack and their walls will crumble.
6	**Their empires will not last.**
9	The world they tried to weave
	will fall apart like rotted fabric.

7	**But the reign of God rolls on forever.**
8	**When the greedy have gone, who will inherit their wealth?**
	Only the poor and brokenhearted will be left.

10	Take heed, you who pursue power at any price!
11	**Serve God, not your own ambitions.**
	Come to God in fear and trembling.

James Taylor

12   **Learn God's ways,**
before God puts you out with the garbage.
The orphans adopted into God's family
will inherit the household.

PSALM 3
Safe from the scavengers

*Themes of vengeance—often violent vengeance—are common in
the psalms. Today, we prefer to think of a God of compassion
and reconciliation. But if we're going to be realistic, we need to
recognize that desire for revenge.*

1   The hyenas bare their teeth;
they snarl all around me.
2   People say, "No one but God can save you now."

3   **You grow around me like a sturdy hedge;**
its bright blossoms shelter me behind their glory.
4   **I cry out to you;**
you answer me in the fragrance of your flowers.
5   **You protect me.**
6   I don't care how the wild beasts snap and snarl
on the far side of the fence.

7   **Drive the rabid curs away, oh Lord!**
Boot them in their bony ribs;
Grind their teeth down to their gums!
8   Then no one need ever fear them again.

For you deliver your people from danger;
you bless your people.

*If you have difficulty imagining God being brutal, remember
that the psalmists didn't sugarcoat their sentiments. They
acknowledged people's emotions—whether or not that's what
God would really do.*

PSALM 3
Unconditional caring

I still remember the rough tweed of my grandfather's jacket, the clean smell of his shaving soap, when he held me in his arms.

1   Everyone is against me.
I can't do anything right.
Friends and relatives snap contradictory commands at me.
2   **They call me useless and incompetent.**
They think I'm a jerk.
They've given up on me. They ignore me.

3   But you never abandon me.
When I am too tired to hold myself up, you carry me.
4   When I skin my knee on life's rough spots,
you reach down and pick me up.
5   **Snuggled in your lap, I can sleep secure;**
with my head on your shoulder, I can safely rest.

6   **As long as I can turn to you,**
I don't care how spiteful others may be.
7   Your voice rumbles, and my persecutors cower;
you wave them away, and they scurry for shelter.
8   Safe in your arms, I look up to you, and you smile at me.
I am so lucky!

         James Taylor

PSALM 4
At home

I travel a lot. Sometimes I stay in cold, impersonal, mass-produced hotel rooms, sometimes in people's homes. Waking in the darkness in an unfamiliar place is always a bit upsetting.

1   In the middle of the night, Lord, I wake.
This room is strange;
I can't find the light; I can't find the door.
2   **I am afraid.**

3   Then I remember—this is your house, God.
I was a stranger, and you took me in.
I was alone, and you made me welcome.
4   **In your house, I have nothing to fear.**
I can sink back into my bed and set my mind at rest.
5   **I put myself in your hands. I trust you.**
6   Am I crazy? Am I a fool?
Some would say so. They doubt you.
7 **But I know the peace I felt when you opened your door**
and the warmth when you invited me to share your table.
8   **I can let my anxious eyelids close again.**
In your home, I am at home.

PSALM 5:1–8
A sense of safety

When our children had nightmares, we held them in our arms until their fears evaporated.

1   Oh my God, hear me.
I'm crying out to you.
2   Listen to my whimpering in the night.
You are not afraid of the blackness,
        so I call for you.

3   You hear my cries, and come to me.
Before dawn wipes away the darkness,
I drowse comfortably in your arms.

4   You are as open as the daylight;
no deceitful thought crosses your mind.
You will not associate yourself with anything underhanded.
5   **Those who brag of their own powers**
reveal their inner emptiness;
you give them enough rope
and they tie themselves in knots.
6   **Anyone who lies to you risks destruction,**
for you do not like being deceived.

7   **Because you are honest and open,**
I know I have a place in your heart.
I live in awe of you;
I reach out my arms towards you.
8   Pick me up and take me with you.
I want to go with you, wherever you are.

PSALM 5:1–8
Wait for the morning

1   Hear me, God!
Hear my lament!
2   Listen to my cry, my creator and companion,
for I have only you to call to in the darkness of my night.

3   **Like the light coming in the east, you hear my voice;**
like the dawn warming a sullen sky,
you respond to my need.
4   **For you will not tolerate wrong.**
5 Those who shoot off their mouths shoot themselves down in flames.
6 **Those who tell lies are trapped by their own deceptions;**
in their lust and licentiousness, they stand naked before you.
They deserve their fate.

7   But I know I will always be welcome,
not because I deserve it,
but because of your motherly love.
So I honor you; I bow my head in awe of you.
8   **Guide me, oh thou great Jehovah,**
lead me safely through the night.

PSALM 8
Awe and wonder

1   My God, my God,
how wonderful you are!
There is nothing like you in the whole earth.

I look up to the skies, and I see you there;
2   **Babies and infants open their mouths,**
and I hear them cry your name.
Compared to you, our weapons, our bombs,
our power to destroy,
dwindle into insignificance.
3 **On a starry night, with your glory splashed across the skies,**
I gaze into your infinite universe, and I wonder:
4   **Who am I?**
Why do I matter?
Why do you care about mere mortals?

We humans are less than specks of dust in your universe.
We have existed less than a second in the great clock of creation.
5   **Yet you choose us as your partners.**
You share the secrets of the universe with us;
you give us a special place in your household;
6   you trust us to look after the earth, on your behalf—
7   **not just the sheep and oxen,**
but also the wolves that prey on our domestic animals;
8 **the birds, the plants, and even creatures we have never seen**
in the depths of the sea.
9   My God, my God! How amazing you are!

PSALM 8:1–6, 9
Friendship flowers

1   Oh God, my God, what a glorious gift you have given.
Above the marvels of nature rises the miracle of friendship.
2   Friends take time for each other;
they put their lives in each other's hands.
Even among thieves there is honor.
3   **Stars and nebulas are far away,**
but friends are near at hand.

4   Friendship flowers unpredictably;
the desert blossoms, the ice melts, the distance disappears.
5   **Friendship has no parallel in the world.**
Envy and jealousy dissolve; fear and suspicion evaporate.

This is how God meant the world to be.
6   **Nothing compares with the wonder of friendship.**
It is not possible with the beasts of the field
or the creatures of the forests,
with the fish of the sea, or the birds of the air.

9   Oh, Lord, our Lord, what a glorious gift you have given!

PSALM 9:9–20
Just desserts

9   Those who are in trouble know where they can turn;
those who are shut out know where they belong.
10   They put their trust in you, God.
They know you will not disappoint them.

11   God, your aura of holiness envelops the earth.
From your universal vantage point,
you keep an eye on everyone.
12   You watch out for all who suffer.

13 **And I, Lord, I am one of those who suffer;**
   be kind to me too.
 Can't you see what those who hate me are doing to me?
   I feel like dying.
14 **Save me, so that I can sing your praises,**
   so that I can stand tall again,
  and tell everyone how you saved me.

15 **Let the high and mighty paint themselves into a corner—**
16 they had all the aces, but they played them wrong.
17   **They weep and wail,**
 because they failed to include God in their calculations.
17 Evil people destroy themselves by their own deceit.
  They chose to ignore God—let them go to hell!
18   God outsmarted their power plays.
   God chose not to play their game.
 But those who are really in need will not be forgotten;
   They will not be left without hope.
19   Show yourself, Lord!
 Judge those who parade pompously before you;
20   **Put the fear of God into them;**
 make them see that they are mere mortals,
   and only you are God.

PSALM 10
Preying on innocence

1   Where have you gone to, God?
  Why can't I see you in this gloom?

2 The weasels have come out of their holes.
 They stalk us in the shadows; they nip and gnaw at us.

3 They claim they can do whatever they want;
  There is nothing to stop them, they say.
4   They say, "God will never see this."
 They argue, "There is no God anyway."

5 The trouble is that they get away with it.
They make a profit—they are sought for their wisdom.
6 **They are convinced that they have all the answers,
for all people, everywhere, all the time.**

7, 8 But their words turn people against each other.
They see everyone as lambs waiting to be fleeced.
9 They have beady eyes and a single agenda—
they wait for lambs to gambol within reach.
10 **Their sharpened teeth gleam.**
When they pounce, who can shake them off?
We are helpless and they are relentless.
They think they can get away with their greedy deeds.
11 **"God does not care," they say.**
"God cannot see our dealings in the dark."

12 **Rise up, oh Lord, like dawn over a darkened world.**
Reveal their deadly deeds and send them scurrying.
13 **They don't believe it will happen;**
they think they are safe from you.

14 But you do see! Your light pierces hidden corners.
You warm the chill of fear, and comfort shivering sufferers.

15 Chase the weasels back into their holes, Lord!
Wall them into their warrens;
make them prowl their maze of darkness through eternity.
16 **Show them who's in charge.**

17 Lord, be faithful with those who have been faithful to you.
Give us courage to continue.
18 Be fair to those who have been cheated by life
so that they may live without fear.

James Taylor

PSALM 10:12–18
Off the bottom

When our economy crashes, we lash out at politicians, expecting them to do something about it. When our spirits break, we turn to God with the same feelings.

12   Get up, God.
                Don't just sit there.
           Don't ignore those who suffer.

13   **Some people say,**
     "I can do what I want. There is no God—
        and if there is, God doesn't care."

14   But you do care.
   Those who struggle can relax in your hands;
   those who are bereft and lonely can depend on you.
   Trouble and sorrow call you into action;
   they tell you it's time to get your hands dirty.

15   **Do something decisive, God.**
        Get tough with your detractors;
   Make them as miserable as they make others.

16   Show them you're the boss.

   Your foes will fade away; no one will remember them.
17   Forget them.
     Turn your attention to the poor, the meek,
            the brokenhearted.

18   **Let the widows, the orphans, the strangers,**
     know that they can expect justice.
     Let them live their lives without fear.

PSALM 13
From a hospital bed

1 How long, oh Lord, must I lie here?
Will you ignore me forever?
2 How long must I struggle along on my own?
My body aches all over;
My own organs wage war against me.
Will you let them win?
How long can I keep up this battle?
How long can I keep on fighting?

3 **Listen to me, God!**
In the dead of night, answer me or let me die!
4 **Then my illness can rejoice for it has triumphed over me;**
it has killed both of us.

5 **Ah, but I trust you, Lord.**
Whatever happens, I know that I am safe in your love.
There is nothing more I could ask, living or dead.
6 So I will praise you, whatever happens.

PSALM 14
The gamble of faith

*A philosopher once argued that if you gamble there is no God,
and there is, you will have lost everything. If you gamble there is
a God, and there isn't, you will have lost nothing. But if you
gamble there is a God, and there is, you will win everything.*

1 Only fools say, "There is no God."
They only fool themselves.
Their actions reveal their delusion;
whatever they do turns out badly.
2 There is a God, who knows what they are doing.

**God loves those who seek justice, show mercy,
and walk humbly with their maker.**

3   But those who turn their backs on God will lose their way;
they stumble over their own shadows.

4   Can't they see what fools they're making of themselves?
They crunch down people's dreams like popcorn;
they grow fat on others' famine.
They deny the reality of God.

5   When they discover their error,
they will dissolve into putrid puddles.
They have challenged God and they cannot win.

6   But we must trust our God;
we have nothing else to rely on.

7   God, save us from those who prey upon us.
**Topple the proud from their pedestals,
and let us trust each other again.**
Then all your people will be glad.

PSALM 15
House rules

*The psalms sometimes convey a certain self-righteousness, as if
the speakers were patting themselves on the back for having
obeyed all the rules. I prefer to think of it as awareness of
ideals—whether or not the speaker measures up.*

1   Who are your preferred guests, Lord?
Who is welcome to stay with you?

2   God seeks those who can hold their heads high,
who have good motives and no hidden agendas.
3   They will not delight in malicious gossip
or relish someone else's problems.

They do not hold grudges.
4 **They do not pursue the patronage of the powerful**
nor the friendship of the foul in spirit.
But they respect those who love God,
who are prepared to sacrifice their own interests
for the sake of others.
5 **They put their wealth to worthwhile use;**
they will not exploit those who cannot protect themselves.

Those who live by these principles
are always welcome in the home of the Lord.

PSALM 15
Hospitality

1 Your doors are always open, God;
you have no locks or fences.
2 Anyone can walk in—
anyone who does no harm to others,
who holds no grudges,
who rejects pretense and sham.
3 Your guests have no double standards.
They will not double-cross a friend for their own gain,
nor sow dissension among their colleagues.
4 **Yet they do not simply tolerate everything.**
They steer clear of evil causes;
they keep their word—even at personal sacrifice.
5 They do not use money merely as a means of making more;
they will not try to profit from the poor and the powerless.
They are not fickle or changeable.
They would never do anything
to cut themselves off from your company.

PSALM 16
The brevity of life

Our family lost four close relatives and an old friend during a single six-week period. It made us acutely aware of human mortality.

1   Life is short, Lord.
       Like a breath in the night, it sinks into silence.
2   Human relationships all pass away;
       we cannot count on them for comfort in old age.
           Only you, God, are forever.
       Why should I put anything else first in my life?

3   Some people hold you as their closest companion.
       They are the saints.
       I would like to be like them.
4   Many people claim to put you first,
       but they chase riches and popularity, privilege and power.
5   I say that there is nothing in life but God.
       You are all anyone needs.

7   In the silence of the night, I listen for the breath of God;
       in the bedlam of a busy day, I wait for whispers of wisdom.
8   I keep my mind on God.
       You surround me like the air I breathe;
           you buoy me up like water.
9   **Even in a time of loss, I raise my arms to your embrace;**
           my heart rests easy.

10   For you are a loving God.
       Though our lives end, we do not vanish into a lifeless void.
11   You gather us into your eternal warmth,
       where we will enjoy the endless sunshine of your smile.

PSALM 17:1–7, 15
The defendant pleads "Not Guilty"

1 Let me present my case, Lord;
Listen to what I have to say.
2 I tell the truth; my lips do not lie.
When you hear my story, you will know I am in the right;
3 You have the wisdom to see through any pretence.
Check up on me, any hour of the day or night.
Test me, and you will find my motives pure—
my words and my actions prove my integrity.
4 I have walked the straight and narrow path;
I have not strayed from the route you marked out for me.

6 I trust you to be fair, God.
Show me that I am right to rely on you.
7 You have a reputation for helping those who turn to you
to escape from their enemies.

9 **The prosecution has piled up evidence against me;**
I am under attack from all sides.
8 **Please, give me special treatment, God.**
Give me the benefit of any doubt.
Treat me like a trusted friend...

15 I rest my case.
I am confident that you will be fair.

PSALM 19:1–6
Scientific study

1 "The heavens declare the glory of God,
and the firmament showeth his handiwork..."
2 The whole earth is God's textbook.
From the edges of the atmosphere
to the core of the planet,
the wonders of the world expand our understanding.

3   **Rocks have no words, nor do cells have syllables,**
4   **yet their message can be read anywhere.**
5   Even the fiery stars, racing through space,
6   yield their secrets to those whose minds
    are open to the mysteries of God's universe.

PSALM 19:7–14
Interdependence

7   An underlying harmony,
a delicate equilibrium built on the value of every thing,
binds together past, present, and future.
8   **There are no exceptions.**
No one is above the universal law of interdependence.
Nothing stands alone.
9   Life dies and becomes new life.
Spirit and flesh are one.
My life is inextricably linked to yours,
and our common survival is tied to the trees and insects.

10   This is the beginning of wisdom.
It is better than wealth, more valuable than possessions.
11   Awareness of it will change you forever.

12   **But we are too often deaf;**
we close our ears to the voices of the winds and waves,
to the insights of the rocks and the plants.
13   God, keep us from thinking we know it all—
an assembly of facts does not equal truth.
Human minds cannot encompass eternity.
14 **Keep us always open to wonder, to beauty, and to mystery,**
oh greatest of mysteries.

PSALM 19:7–14
A celebration of curiosity

When I had to memorize Psalm 19 as a child, I thought of the laws of God as a straitjacket that restricted freedom. But God's laws are written in creation—they keep the universe running.

Insight and understanding, excitement and discovery, grow as we explore the precepts and principles of God's universe.

7   The ways of the Lord are wonderful.
With sure skill, God has woven the web of life.
8   Predictable patterns emerge;
we recognize them and rejoice.
The laws of the universe
unfold like a flower before our thirsting minds;
we begin to understand.
9   Our intellects explore the fabric of a planet pulsing with life.
We sense the underlying order of the universe—
it is so true, so right, that we stand in awe.
10 **These insights are worth more than wealth and popularity,**
more than chocolate kisses or honeyed words.
11   **By them we come to understand our place;**
Within this pattern we find our role and responsibility.

12   **Yet pride seduces us into considering ourselves special.**
13   Keep us from presuming our own importance, God;
protect us from those who promote selfish, short-sighted goals.
Then we can be innocent of crimes against your tapestry of life.

14   **Let all that I learn and all that I do
be acceptable to you, Lord of all life.**

PSALM 20
For a child leaving home

I wish I had known this psalm when our daughter Sharon moved to Alberta. This is the blessing I would like to have given her.

1   God bless you, my child.
As you set out into the world, God go with you;
every step of every day, God watch over you.
2   **When you're feeling low, may God send you**
a shoulder to cry upon,
a friendly hand to help you up.
3   **When you're feeling good,**
may your laughter echo in the heavens.
Whatever you do, may it be acceptable in God's sight.
4   **May God hear the deepest yearnings of your heart**
and help those buds of hope blossom into reality.
5   **May the word we hear of you always be good.**
Then we will know
that you knew God while you were growing up,
and that God still belongs in your new life.
May you remember how to pray,
6   **for God will not desert those who stay in touch.**

7   Some of your new friends will put their faith in money,
others in power, and some in fast cars.
Put your faith only in the Lord our God.
8 **Those who put their faith in false gods will stumble and fall.**
But you will not be afraid of the light;
you can stand straight and tall.

9   Lord, into your hands we commit our child.
Take her under your wing,
for our sakes, and for yours.

PSALM 21:1-7
The foundation of life

Have you ever noticed that the so-called "self-made man" claims credit only when "he" is successful? When such people fail, they have no one to blame but themselves.

1 None of us achieves anything on our own account.
We succeed only with your help, oh holy one.

2 What we have wanted, you put within our grasp;
we asked for it, and you gave it.

3 You gave each of us as many abilities as we need;
to each of us, you measured out 24 hours a day.

4 We asked for life and you gave it to us—
three score years and ten.
**And if by chance it should be more,
our length of life depends on your discretion—**
it is not our own doing.

5 **If we achieve fame, it is with your help;**
if we are given honors, they are your gift.

6 **Gentle contentment wreathes the faces
of those who walk with you as their daily companion;**
they are blessed by your presence.

7 **In everything, we know that we can trust you;**
if you are with us, who can be against us?
You make us worthwhile.

PSALM 22:1–15
Utter depression

In the depths of a crisis, people do not have the energy to struggle for socially acceptable phrases. They do not mince their words when they cry out.

1 My God, my God—are you deaf and blind?
I expected you to help me, to ease my anguish!
2 For God's sake, God! Do something!
All day long, I pour out my pain.
All night long, I cower from my fears.
Alone, God, all alone.

3 **My parents told me I could trust you.**
4 Their parents trusted you, they said,
and you came through for them.
5 **They cried out to you in the old days, and they were saved.**
They trusted you, and you didn't let them down.

6 **But not me. You've forgotten me.**
I am a cockroach, crawling in the corners,
waiting to be stepped on.
Some people scorn me, others try to stomp on me.
7 **Everyone makes fun of me.**
They crack jokes at my expense;
they suck their teeth, they shake their heads.
8 "If God is really on your side," they scoff,
"why won't God rescue you?
Doesn't your God bother keeping promises?"

9 And yet I cannot forget—you shaped me in my mother's womb;
you rocked me in my mother's arms;
10 you taught me how to crawl.
Since I was a child,
you have been as close to me as the air I breathe.
11 Do not let me suffocate now for lack of air.
For God's sake, help me!

12   I feel as if I am sealed inside a plastic bag.
It clings to my face; I cannot breathe.
13   It distorts my vision.
I see my tormentors dancing around me—
14   it is like looking at them through running water.
I wilt like a seedling in the summer sun.
My bones cannot support me. They soften like warm wax;
my spirits sag.
15   My throat chokes with dust;
it glues my tongue to the roof of my mouth.
I might as well be dead.

PSALM 22:1–18
Abandoned

1   Alone—I'm all alone.
There is no God; there are no friends;
I'm all alone.
2   **I call all day, but no one calls me back;**
I cry all night, but no one comforts me.
3   **Could God create a world this rotten?**
Could any God call this good?
4   **Our ancestors were deluded.**
They trusted God;
they thought God changed the course of history for them—
5   they actually believed it!
6   **With scientific detachment, I know that I am nothing.**
Nothing I do makes any difference.
7   **Universes and social systems roll inexorably onward;**
they mock my pathetic struggles;
8   **they laugh at my lofty ideals.**

9   Yet still I talk to you, as if you were real.
I argue with you, as if you had a mind to change.
From the moment of my conception,
I have sensed your will surrounding me
like the waters of my mother's womb.

10   **You are my umbilical cord, my source of life.**

12   The ways of the world seduce me;
    with honeyed visions they draw me downwards.
13   I would run in fear from a raging lion,
    but I cannot resist the lure of luxury.
14   **I would brace myself, but my bones turn to jelly;**
    I would stand tall, but I melt into a puddle.
15   **Like a fleck of fluff, I am blown about by every breeze.**

16   When the sun comes out, I will dry up;
    when the wind roars, I will vanish into the night.
    I will not exist any more.
17   **I am nothing.**
18   Nothing that I have done, and nothing I have achieved,
    will outlive me.

PSALM 22:16–22
A last gasp

16   The hyenas skulk around, waiting for me to die;
    vultures hunch overhead.
    I cannot protect myself any longer.
17   **The vultures will pick my bones bare;**
    the hyenas are already salivating over my corpse.
18   **Nothing of me will survive this crisis;**
    Even my clothing will be ripped to shreds.

19   **Don't shrug a cold shoulder at my plight, God.**
    Don't leave me to perish in my misery!
20   **Free me from the thorns that pin me down;**
    from the constant clamor of negative thoughts
    racing relentlessly through my mind,
    release me!

21   **I'm desperate, God!**
    The jaws of the carrion eaters are closing on my flesh;

their hot breath reeks in my nostrils.
The maggots are lining up to feast on my mutilated carcass.

22 **Save me! And I will give you the credit forever.**
I will never stint in your praise.

PSALM 22:23–31
Saintly sacrifice

A friend walked with not one but three AIDS victims down, as Shakespeare put it, "the way to dusty death."

23 Behold a saint!
Few could do what she does:
she goes down to the hospice, every day,
24 where people waste away with AIDS.
She does not hide her face behind a mask,
nor her hands inside rubber gloves.
When they cry in misery, she cradles them in her arms.

25 We shake our heads in awe at such selfless service.

26 **She feeds them, spoonful by spoonful.**
They watch with sunken burning eyes;
they turn their skintight skulls and kiss her cheek.
27 Their own families turn away from them;
long after those sons and brothers have died,
after those daughters and sisters have passed away,
their survivors will remember her devotion.
28 In her they see God's kind of love;
love that has no limits and sets no conditions.
29 God's love does not distinguish
between the froth on the top and the dregs on the bottom;
it makes no distinctions
between the lords and the lepers of our society.
30 Years from now, people will speak of her visits in hushed voices;
they will hold her high as an example to follow.
31 Because of her, they will know God better.

PSALM 22:25–31
The Lord of all life

25   In every part of the world, there are those who praise you.
They form a great congregation of the faithful.
26   And this is their sign—
their poor no longer go to bed hungry,
their weak are protected, their strangers welcomed.
God gives life to the forgotten!
27   From the river deltas to the mountain tops,
from the rain forests to the ice caps,
all nations, all peoples, all creation
live and breathe in praise of the Creator.
28   **For in the end, everything comes back to God;**
The Lord is incarnate in all life.
29   **Fat moles that burrow in the earth**
and swallows that fly above it,
sleek tuna that swim the oceans
and steel tankers that furrow the seas,
all owe their origin to God the Creator.
None are self-sufficient;
they will all decay into dust,
except as they live on in the Lord.
30   As they teach their children about the mystery,
their successors will also serve the Lord.
31   **Thus the Lord touches generations waiting to be born,**
and transcends the tyranny of time.

PSALM 23
Mommy holds my hand

The only way to paraphrase such a familiar psalm is to take a totally different metaphor that still conveys the wonderful sense of trust of the original. One image that came to me was a small child walking down the street holding its mother's hand.

1   God is like my Mommy.
My Mommy holds my hand;
I'm not afraid.

2   **She takes me to school in the mornings;**
she lets me play in the playgrounds and the parks;

3   **she makes me feel good.**
She shows me how to cross the streets,
because she loves me.

4   **Even when we walk among the crowds and the cars,**
I am not afraid.
If I can reach her hand or her coat,
I know she's with me,
And I'm all right.

5   When I fall down and I'm all covered with mud
and I come home crying,
she picks me up in her arms.
She wipes my hands and dries my tears,
and I have to cry again,
because she loves me so much.

6   How can anything go wrong
with that kind of Mommy near me?
I want to live all my life with Mommy,
in my Mommy's home for ever and ever.

PSALM 23
Looking back on a full life

During a memorial service, John Smith suggested that Psalm 23 could have been written by an older person, reflecting on a long and full life. The first line of verse 6 is adapted from "A New Creed" of the United Church of Canada.

1   God has walked with me; I could ask nothing more.
2   **God has given me green meadows to laugh in,**
clear streams to think beside, untrodden paths to explore.

3   When I thought the world rested on my shoulders,
God put things into perspective.
When I lashed out at an unfair world, God calmed me down.
When I drifted into harmful ways, God straightened me out.
God was with me all the way.

4   I do not know what lies ahead, but I am not afraid.
I know you will be with me.
Even in death, I will not despair.
You will comfort and support me.
5   Though my eye dims and my mind dulls,
you will continue to care about me.
Your touch will soothe the tension in my temples;
my fears will fade away.
I am content.

6   **In life, in death, in life beyond death, God is with me.**
All through life, I have found goodness in people.
When life ends, I expect to be gathered
into the ultimate goodness of God.

PSALM 23
Blessed relief

*After a day of chasing through shopping malls, Psalm 23 took on
a new significance.*

1   God keeps a cool café. What more could I ask?
2   **She provides a comfortable chair
to take the weight off my weary feet;**
she puts up an umbrella to shade me from the sun;
3   **she serves me iced tea.**

4 Though I have battled with the crowds at the bargain counters,
though I have suffered the scent of too many sweaty bodies,
I don't care.
5   **I know what's waiting for me at the end of the day.**
An ice cream cone.
It drips over the edges, and I lick it up gratefully.
I close my eyes;
the sound system plays the gentle chuckles of waves
lapping on a shore.
6   **I am content.**
I would love to sit here forever.
In God's cool café.

PSALM 24
Earth-rise

*When astronauts first showed us our planet from the moon, they
changed our theology forever.*

1   Turning and turning, our pale blue globe
burns bright in the blackness of eternity.
**The Earth is the Lord's, and all that is in it—
all life embodied in the only home we know.**
2   God created life in the oceans,
and nourishes it with nutrients from the mountains.

        James Taylor

3   Trace the course of a river to its source;
stand among the mountains and marvel.
Who would dare defile this paradise?

4   **God sees through our deceit and pretense;**
we cannot claim innocence when we have dirty hands.
We can only approach God with clean hands and pure hearts.

5   Then we will see a smile on the face of God;
then God's wisdom will be evident in the world.

6   So seek the Lord in high and holy places.

7   **Let the vast valleys throw open their arms,**
let the summits stand tall in pride,
For this is the body of our God!

8   With all the glory of the universe to choose from,
with all of creation quivering in expectation,
the Lord of life picked this planet as home.

9   **So throw open your valleys, oh earth!**
Spread wide your plains to welcome the Lord!

10   **For the Lord of all creation lives here.**

PSALM 25:1–9
Negotiating with God

Abraham bargained with God to try to save the people of Sodom. Moses talked God out of destroying the Israelites, by persuading God that the Egyptians would consider God a failure if the Israelites died in the desert. Obviously, it's okay to use negotiating skills in talking with God.

1   To you, my Lord, I plead my case.

2   I trust you; don't let me make a fool of myself.

3   **You wouldn't humiliate your loyal helpers, would you?**
Save your heavy hand for those who don't care about you.

4   **I want to be your friend, Lord.**
I want to do things your way.

5   So take my hand,
and guide me through the potholes and pitfalls of life.
You are the only one who can save me;
You are what I have been looking for, all my life.

6   **Don't do it just for my sake.**
Do it for your own reputation as a loving God.

7   **Don't count my past mistakes against me.**
Be true to yourself—
you are a loving God, so show me love, oh Lord.

8   **Lord, because you are perfect,**
you can take pity on less perfect people;

9   You can train us how to follow your example.
Don't just condemn us—give us a chance!

PSALM 25:1–10
Set a good example

1   I'm following your footsteps, my Savior.
I trust you. Do not mislead me.

2   **Don't draw me into difficulties**
where others can crow over my humiliation.

3   Let those who are sneaky and devious
make fools of themselves, Lord.

4   But I do not want to be one of them.
I want to be like you.

5   Hold my hand while I learn to walk.
You are my only chance;
I hang all my hopes on you.

6   I've been told you don't hold grudges;
I have heard you are compassionate.

7   Don't hold my stumbling against me.
I have done wrong—but who hasn't?
Except you.
If you must judge, set us an example;

show us the compassion and kindness
you expect us to show others.
8 Act according to your standards, not the world's.
9 **Then the humble will learn how to handle themselves,**
the broken of body will be able to stand straight,
and the poor can walk proud,
10 **because they walk in your ways.**
Your way is founded on love and faithfulness.
Those who walk with you, learn from you.

PSALM 26:1–12
A faithful lover

Nothing rankles more than unfair criticism. We character-
istically respond by overstating our defense.

1 Do not reject me, God. I have been true to you.
I have trusted you;
I have never doubted you for more than a moment.
2 **If you don't believe me, test me.**
Look into my heart and listen to my thoughts.
See for yourself that I have been faithful.

3 Can't you see that your love means everything to me?
Everything I do, I do for you.
4 I don't play around with pretense;
I don't flirt with false ideals.
5 I despise those who do wrong;
I avoid those who flaunt their faithlessness.
6 **I wash my hands of them.**
My hands are clean;
I come to you with a clear conscience.
7 I constantly count my blessings;
I always speak well of you.
I bless the day you entered my life.
8 **I glow when I am near you;**
I bask in the sunshine of your smile.

9   Don't look at me like something rotting
in the back of the fridge;
don't dump me out with your garbage.
10   The trash can is full of people who cheat and swindle;
they deceive their friends;
they play both ends against the middle.

11   But I am not like them.
12   I can hold my head high,
because I have been faithful to you.

PSALM 27:1, 4–9
My only hope

4   All I ever wanted was peace and harmony.
I would love to live serenely in God's presence.
Instead of protecting me from the tragedies of life
God gives me ways to cope with them.
1   **When wild-eyed beasts glare at me out of the gloom,**
God gives me fire;
its flames keep my fears at bay.
5   **When rival demands clash like bloodied boxers,**
God sends a breeze to blow away
the swirling dust of strife.
6   When I can see clearly again,
I know I don't want to fight anyone.
I would rather praise the one who saves me.

7   Don't stop now, Lord.
When fearsome monsters lurk under the surface of my mind,
come to my rescue.
8   "Turn to me," you say. "Do things my way."
From the bottom of my heart, God, I have turned to you.
9   Don't turn away from me.
You are my only hope.

PSALM 27:1-6
Nothing to fear

The same week that a friend was to be married, she was diagnosed with cancer. What should have been a week of joy became a week of worries.

1 In the darkness of the night I lie awake and tremble.
But with the dawn, fears fade away.
When I can see with my own eyes
that there is nothing to be afraid of,
why should I fear?
**If I could see with God's eyes,
I would know I have nothing to fear.**
2 No, even if scalpels carve up my flesh,
even if therapies poison my body,
I have nothing to fear.
Malignant forces that might harm me will surely self-destruct;
By their own rapacious appetites, they will consume themselves.
3 **Though fate stacks the deck against me,
I will not despair.**
Though tumors grow within me,
I will remain confident,
as long as you are with me.

4 I have only one desire, one goal in life:
I want to be part of your family.
I want to look along the festive table
and touch the bonds of kinship—
with my cousins, my ancestors, my descendants.
5 **Within that family I can feel safe.**
I can hide my face in my mother's skirts,
and rest my head on my son's shoulder.
6 Within that family, I need no longer fear;
I can sing and dance;
I can be the joyful woman you created.

PSALM 27:7–14
Waiting to be found

A little lost dog huddled under a hedge at the corner of our block, waiting for someone to find it. (The ancient Hebrew of the Psalms used the same word for "wait" and "hope.")

7
I raise my head and howl at the sky.
Hear my cry, and come to me!

8
"Where is your home?" my heart pounds;
"You are lost, you are lost, you are lost!"
I need to find my master.
Find me, master! Do not forget me!

9
Do not be angry with me for wandering away;
do not punish me for straying from your side.
You taught me, you trained me;
Now show me you can save me, too.

10
When I was small, you took me into your home;
You took me for your very own.

11
Do not desert me now, when I have lost my way
taking paths you did not teach me.

12
Do not abandon me to an alien world
where I can trust no one.
I fear for my life.

13
I will lie down here and wait.
Soon I will hear my master's voice calling me;
I will see familiar feet coming towards me.

14
I can be brave, if I know help is coming.
I shall lie down here, and wait.

PSALM 28
A mighty oak

We huddled under a huge tree for shelter from a rain squall.
Standing there, we slowly became aware of the number of other
creatures that lived their lives in and around that tree and its
massive roots.

1 Beneath your mighty limbs, God, I huddle for shelter.
Stretch your branches over me;
Let me cling to your rugged roots,
to keep from being whirled away like the last leaves of autumn.
2 **I wrap my arms around you;**
I press my cheek against your immovable might.
3 **Do not let invisible winds steal me away.**
Their fingers pluck at my clothes;
they promise adventure and excitement.
But they have no substance; they lure me to destruction.
4 Treat them as they deserve.
5 **They puff themselves up.**
Because they cannot be held or grasped,
they think they are a law unto themselves.
Without you, they are but a dying breath,
a sigh that stirs the dust, and then is known no more.

6 **Thank you, God.**
7 **Beneath your branches, we are safe.**
We see you reaching up to touch the sky,
and feel ourselves uplifted.
8 **Your strength becomes our strength.**
You are our shelter from the storm.
9 **Protect us, and watch over us,**
and we will stay in your shade forever.

PSALM 29
When the storm strikes

We tend to grow complacent about our own capabilities—until a hurricane roars in from the ocean, or a flood surges down the valley, or a forest fire rages out of control.

1   Trust God—don't pin your faith on human potential.
2   **Science and technology, wealth and popularity—**
        these will all pass away.
      Only God is worthy of lasting worship.
3 **Fame and fortune will not save you when the tempest strikes.**
    The winds whirl in; waves crash upon your comfortable shore.
4   **Houses collapse like cards;**
    corporations crumble; assets become worthless.
5   Branches break off; mighty empires are uprooted.
    Possessions, wealth, and status cannot save you.
8   You stand alone before the power of God,
    as naked and helpless as the day you were born.
6   **You tremble like a twig in a tempest.**
9   All that you depended upon is stripped away,
    like the last leaves from autumn trees.
10   **Before God's power, you face your own frailty.**
    Nothing can save you—except God.
11   Only God is greater than any human crisis.
    Only God can sustain you through the storm,
    and carry you to the calm on the other side.

PSALM 29
Riding on God's shoulders

We used to take our children to the big exhibition each summer. We held on to them tightly, to keep them from getting lost in the crowds.

1   Age and experience have their benefits.
2 A child's excitement sometimes needs a parent's stability.

3   **A caring parent is like a raft in a torrent of people.**
The flood surges along irresistibly.
4   **It picks up small children
and swirls them away under its surface.**
5   Its bedlam drowns the tiny cries of lost little ones.
The calls of parents go unheard.
6   But a child is safe, riding on a parent's shoulders.
It rises above the tumult; it cannot be swept away.

7   God, you stand firm against every tumult.
No flood can tumble you along;
no crisis can sweep you away.
8   **Sometimes we cannot hear your voice over the chaos;**
the din of destruction drowns our feeble cries for help.
**We can be safe only when we wrap our arms around your neck,
and hold you tight.**
9   Then the torrent cannot touch us.
11 **God is much stronger than we are.**
God can carry us to safety.

PSALM 30
A second chance

1   My life has turned around.
2, 3   **God has shown me a better way to live.**
I know how it feels to be down and out;
I know doubt and depression too well.
5   But these things are like clouds passing over the sun;
their shadow pales when the light breaks through.
4   Like an alcoholic freed from addiction,
like a prisoner pardoned,
I must tell my tale over and over.

6   **When things went well, I took all the credit.**
7   When things went wrong, I fell apart.
I blamed myself for my failure.
8   I blamed God for punishing me.

I asked God, "Does it make you feel good
to make me feel bad?
9 **Would you rather have me praise you or curse you?**
Who else will people listen to—the dust or the wind?
10 **Give me another chance!"**

11 It worked!
I started feeling better.
I looked for the goodwill around me, instead of the ill;
I quit moping and started dancing.
12 Now I know I owe my good fortune to God,
And I thank God every chance I get.

PSALM 30
Self-discovery

*The greatest liberation for many women is the discovery that
they are not intrinsically inferior to men.*

2 I thought I was born inferior; you gave me self-esteem.
3 **I let others speak for me; I let others think for me.**
I felt I was nothing.
You gave me new life.
4 I am not a faulty copy of anyone else, God.
I am me. Thank you.
5, 7 **Once I thought God despised me.**
But I have felt God's gentle hands lift me into the light.
8 **I cried silently in the night, afraid to be heard.**
I stifled my own suffering.
I thought I didn't matter.
9 **I could have died—but I was afraid no one would notice.**
10 "Can anyone hear me?" I cried. "Does anyone care?"
11 **And you heard me, God.**
You turned my rainclouds into rainbows;
you stirred spices into my watery stew.
12 I am done with self-abasement.
I will delight in me and in you.

PSALM 31:1–5, 15–16
Out on a limb

1   The winds of fate buffet me, Lord.
I cling to you.
2   Gales of temptation try to tear me from my commitments.
I'm being blown away, Lord. I need shelter.
3   Give me something solid to hold onto;
don't let all the effort you put into me go to waste.
4   I went way out on a limb for you, Lord;
now I hear the chainsaws coming.
5   **I can't hang on much longer; I'll have to jump.**
I cast my fate to the winds—
Catch me, please!

15   **My life is in your hands.**
Only you can save me.
16   Free me from the gravity of my situation, Lord;
let my spirit soar like an eagle again.
If you love me, save me!

PSALM 31:9–16
Malicious whispers

9   I feel lousy, Lord.
My head aches, my heart aches, my whole body aches.
10   My life is a sea of suffering.
Night after night, I toss in torment, tangled in my sheets;
I cannot sleep; I waste away with weariness.
12   **My mind has turned to mush.**
I can't get my act together for anything any more.
11   **I have become a laughing stock.**
My colleagues make fun of me, my neighbors avoid me—
even people who pass in the street turn away from me.
13   I hear them whispering about me.
They put their heads together;
behind my back, they plot my humiliation.

14   But they won't make me quit, Lord, for I trust in you.
       I know that you are my God.

15   Even when I can't help myself, you will guard me;
       My survival is safe in your hands.
16   Don't turn away from me too—
       If you love me, restore my confidence.

PSALM 31:19–24
Justified trust

19   I was right to trust you;
       you do not let your friends down.
20   In my arid desert,
       littered with the bleached bones of lost relationships,
           you revived me like a glass of icy lemonade.
21   **In a mall of frozen faces chasing their own concerns,**
       you met me with a broad smile and open arms.
22   I thought I was alone, but I wasn't.
23   **You never forget your friends, God.**
       Only those who choose complete self-sufficiency
           find themselves left to their own resources.

24   **Anyone who feels out on a limb, take heart!**
       Maybe you're looking for salvation in the wrong place.
       Look to your God, and you'll never be alone.

PSALM 32
Confessional

A friend, a Roman Catholic, once said, "You Protestants have no idea how good it feels to be able to confess something and get it off your chest!"

1   Happy are those who have nothing to hide;
2   **Even happier those whose slate has been wiped clean.**
3   I used to lie awake, worrying about things I had done;
    and during the day, about things I had not done.
4   My conscience tormented me. I couldn't concentrate.
    I was terrified of being exposed.

5   So I went to God, and confessed.
    I made no excuses for myself; I didn't hide anything.
6   And God forgave me.
    What a relief it is to share a gnawing secret!
7   Forgiveness is like a cool drink on a hot day,
    like a warm fire in a winter blizzard.
    God's grace renews my strength;
    it gives me a second chance.

8   God says, "I will teach you how to take charge of your behavior.
9   **You are not like horses and camels**
    who need bridles and bits to control them.
10 You have a mind; you can think.
    You can anticipate consequences before you act."
11 Experience isn't always the best teacher.
    Let God lead you through life.

PSALM 33:1–3
A new kind of song

1   If you're on the Lord's side, be glad!
        If you live in the light, thank God!
2   **Shout it and sing it, live it and look it;**
        play your melody of praise in every element of life.
3   **Sing a new song to the Lord,**
        a song composed of all your skills!

PSALM 33:4–9
The circle of life

4   You can depend on God;
        Whatever God does, God does openly.
5   God does not deceive anyone;
        God loves justice; God loves the soul that has no shadows.

6   Look and see—the earth itself shows the nature of God!
        For God created the skies that arch above us;
        everything that lives under those skies
        owes its life to the elements of the air.
        The breath of life is the gift of God.
7   **Clouds form over the oceans, rains shower the hills,**
        and streams return to the sea—
        the source and sustenance of earthly life.

8   Everything begins and ends with God;
        the circle of life is complete.
        What can we do but stand in awe?
9   **However it was done, God did it;**
        according to God's will, it was done,
        and God saw that it was good...

Until now...

PSALM 33:10–22
Our responsibility

10 **We plunder creation to satisfy short-term needs.**
In strip-mined forests, countless species face extinction;
air and water are burdened with wastes;
the earth has been hurt beyond healing.
11 **If only we could hear the wisdom of the Lord.**
Only God can plan beyond the present,
beyond our children, beyond our children's children,
into a seamless tapestry that weaves all life together.
12 **How exciting to perceive that pattern!**
How challenging to be chosen by God
to help preserve an island planet.

13 **God sees all that we do—each one of us.**
No place, no person, no nation can escape God's oversight,
14 **God lives wherever life flowers,**
and dies wherever greed steals from our common future.
15 **God knows what lurks in every heart,**
and weighs each one of us by our works.

16 **We cannot win approval with wealth;**
before God, popularity has no power.
17 **Starships cannot carry us**
from the consequences of our actions—
wherever we go, our attitudes go with us.
18 **But a smile shines on those who struggle**
to live in God's way,
on those who trust God to show them the way.
19 **Even in a wasteland without values,**
they will not work in vain;
God will sustain them.
20 **We rest our hope in God.**
21 We celebrate God's influence in our lives—
living in us, living through us,
offering life to all.
22 We put our trust in God.

PSALM 34:1–8
Rescued!

1   Thank you, God, thank you!
You brought me through my troubled times,
You resurrected me when I had given up hope.

2   Bitter tears kept me awake at night.
God granted me the sweet relief of sleep.
3   I woke refreshed, rejoicing.
4 **I poured out my problems to God; I held nothing back.**
I made no excuses for myself.
God calmed my frantic thoughts,
and untied the knots in my tender muscles.

5   If you put your faith in God,
you can shine like the morning sun;
you need never be ashamed of who you are.
6   I was a worry wart, a hopeless case,
paralyzed by my panic.
But God made something of me.
7 **Those whom God protects live in a bubble of brightness.**
Nothing dulls their shine—
whatever happens, they have an inner beauty that still shimmers.
8   **Open your eyes! See the light!**
Put your faith in God, and find yourself.

PSALM 34:9–14
The wisdom of God

9   Holiness is its own reward;
draw close to the holy one, and see.
10   Sooner or later, every predator becomes prey.
The hunter becomes the hunted, the victor becomes a victim.
But those who learn the wisdom of God
have everything they will ever need.
11   **Hear the wisdom of God in a few words:**
12   **choose life, not death.**
Avoid whatever causes death, to anyone or anything.
13   **Speak the truth, always.**
14   Do good, not evil; seek peace;
instead of anticipating opposition, assume goodwill in others.

PSALM 34:15–22
A very present help

15   God favors those who are honorable and trustworthy;
16   **God rejects those who harm others.**
17   When those who are God's friends need help, God will be there;
18   **God will be especially close**
to those whose dreams have been dashed,
whose hopes have been shattered,
whose hearts have been stabbed.
19   Faith will not free you from troubles,
but it will keep them from conquering you.
21, 22   God watches over those who live their faith;
but those who put their faith in themselves
will find themselves forgotten.

PSALM 34:12–22
Outstretched wings

12   Does anyone want to die young?
Is there anyone who doesn't want a good life?
13   Then mind your mouth and your thoughts.
Don't waste words on worthless gossip;
don't let your lips drip lies.
14 Don't toy with temptation, thinking you can always say "No";
say "No" right now,
and seek God's peace instead of selfish pleasure.

15   God has eagle eyes, to see who's good;
those who please God
nestle into the warmth of God's breast-feathers.
16   But God help those who hurt others,
with their hands or their hearts,
with their words or their wishes.
    In the end, they will wish they had never been born.

17   **When God's little ones fall and hurt themselves,**
God hears their cry, and gathers them with gentle sighs;
with warm salt tears, God bathes away their sorrows.
18   **For God knows how much a broken heart can hurt.**
19   Nest eggs will not prevent pain,
nor investments protect you from abuse.
But when winds lash your fragile wings,
God will fly beside you.
You can ride out the storm together.
20   **Your spirit will not be broken.**

21   Don't take pride in the power of your own wings;
some day, you may come crashing down.
22   Trust only in the overarching wings of the Lord;
no one who runs to God will be turned away.

PSALM 35:17–28
Witness for a victim

When your survival is threatened, it's hard to remember instructions to "turn the other cheek."

17 The spiders spin their webs
and trap me in their sticky deceits;
I struggle to free myself.
How can you sit there like a spectator?
18 Set me free!
Save me, and I'll sing your praises wherever I go.
Any time I have an audience, I'll say a good word for you.
19 **What good am I to you if I'm dead?**
Your foes will laugh in your face.
They'll call you spineless. Gutless. Helpless.
20 **They are troublemakers.**
They pass their poisoned gossip;
like spiders, they watch
while their victims entangle themselves.
21 **They have chosen me as their next victim.**
They claim to have witnessed my crimes.
22 But you see everything.
You are the ultimate eye witness.
23 Stop being a spectator, and speak out!
Let everyone know the truth. Vindicate me!

24 Don't do it for anything I can do for you in return;
do it because of who you are.
25 **Don't let yourself be an accomplice to their arrogance!**
Don't let them believe they have beaten you!
26 **Pull the rug out from under them! Make them look foolish!**
Throw them into confusion, so they start fighting with each other.

27 **Then those who still believe will celebrate.**
They will know that you care about your faithful followers.
28 **And I will put in that good word for you every chance I get.**

PSALMS 36:5–10
Harmony in God's home

5   Your door is always open, God.
You stand at your door, and welcome all who come to it.
6   Entry to your home is not limited
to your friends, your associates, your social class.
You extend your welcome to everyone and everything:
beggars and outcasts, oppressors and victims,
people who have handicaps and drifters who huddle in culverts.
From rats skulking in their sewers
to condors soaring in the clouds—
You make them all welcome.

7   **All of creation is your household, God.**
All can live together in harmony under your roof.
8   **In your kitchens they are fed;**
in your living room, they are entertained and uplifted.
9   **For you are life itself.**
10   Continue to give us life, oh Lord.
Show us how to live in harmony in your home.

PSALMS 37:1–11
Good investments

*Images of God do not have to be agricultural. In today's world,
people are more likely to measure their prosperity economically.*

1   Don't worry that others seem more successful than you.
2   Their short-term gains won't last;
the market will turn against them again.
3   For long-term confidence, invest in God
and count on continuing prosperity and well-being.
4   An unconditional investment in God
can lead to everything you ever wanted,
but could never afford.
5   **But your investment must be unconditional.**

You can't hold anything back;
you can't hedge your bets.
First turn everything over to God—
then you will see how God acts for you. .

6   **You cannot manipulate God for your own gain.**
Make God your manager,
and free yourself forever from cycles of boom and bust.

7a   **Be patient. Wait until God is ready.**

8   Avoid impatience or anger;
they will affect your judgment adversely.

7b   Do not envy those who glory in quick gains
or who profit from crooked practices.

9   **They'll get what they deserve, in God's good time.**

10   In time, corrupt politicians will lose their mandate;
corner-cutting businesses will run out of room;
drug dealers will destroy their brains;
unjust laws will be lifted from the books.
They will all dissipate like morning fog;
you'll wonder how they fostered so much fear for so long.

11 But those who invested their faith in God will continue to flourish;
they will live life abundantly.

PSALM 40:1–11
Lifted out of the mire

1   I believed I could make it on my own.
But I slipped and fell.
I sank into a morass of my own making.

2   God heard my cry.
God lifted me out of the mire and set me on solid ground.

3   Like any convert to a new life,
I must talk about what has happened to me.
I am willing to risk being a bore;
if just one person hears me, my work has not been wasted.

4   **Too many today chase false gods;**
they try to multiply their own gains.

5	But the richest returns come from God.
	You can't begin to count your blessings!

6 God does not want us to wear frowns or long faces;
God wants us to find childlike joy in shining drops of dew,
in whispering pine needles,
in warm mud between the toes.
7, 8 Our delight becomes one with God's;
Our personalities meld.

9 So I will not keep silent;
I will proclaim my good news privately and publicly.
10 **I cannot keep it to myself.**

PSALM 41:1–13
Best friend

Many people still think of God primarily as a judge, handing out punishment for mistakes. But there are other possibilities.

1 If you expect God to treat you kindly,
treat others the same way.
2 **Do not deal harshly with the least of God's little ones,**
and God will not deal harshly with you.
3 God will strengthen you when you're sick;
God will heal your inner wounds,
4 **even if they're self-inflicted.**

For who can claim perfection?
I can't; I have frequently let God down.
5 **My frailty is so obvious,**
even my friends believe God is punishing me.
6 They say nice things to my face,
but behind my back they skewer me with gossip.
7 **They gloat over my misfortunes;**
they tuck their heads together to spread nasty rumors;
they rub their hands in ghoulish glee.

8   It must be cancer, they whisper. Or AIDS.
9   **My closest friends ate and drank with me;**
    now they imagine the worst.

10   **But you will not treat me that way, God.**
    I'm sure of it.
    Get me onto my feet again;
    let me gather my wits once more.
    Then I will show them how little they really know you.
11   **You are my true friend.**
    You will not treat me as they did.
12   **For you never lost faith in me.**
    You countersigned my debts when I was down and out.
    You held my hand when I trembled.
    You gave me strength.
13   **You are my best friend, forever.**
    From the bottom of my heart, I thank you.

PSALM 42
Struggling towards the goal

1   As a long-distance swimmer struggles towards land,
    I struggle towards you, Lord.
2   **I am in danger of drowning.**
    My feet long to rest on solid ground again.
3   Below me the black depths wait pitilessly.

6   **When I feel most hopeless, I turn to you, God.**
    Though I am tossed by swells I cannot see,
    I sense your presence with me through the night.
7   **Even the surf that breaks over me is your creation;**
    the winds and the currents all do your will.
8   **When skies cloud over, though I cannot see the stars,**
    I know that they are there.
    Though I cannot see you, I know that you are there too.

10   **In the gloom, doubts torment me.**
"You believe in God?" they echo in the empty corners of my mind.
"Why doesn't God rescue you?" they demand.
"Why won't God make it easy for you?"

11   **But why am I downcast? Why am I disturbed?**
If God is with me, who can be against me?
So I keep my faith;
and I struggle on.

PSALM 43
Give us a sign

1   The skeptics make fun of my faith;
        they scorn my convictions.
        "There is no God," they claim.
        "Why should we care about right and wrong?"
2   **They laugh at me when I turn to you, my God.**
        When you do not answer,
        they call it confirmation of their charges.
        Why do you let these things happen?
3   We need a sign as unmistakable
        as a searchlight sweeping the darkness;
        all can follow the beam to its luminous source.
4   There, in the white-hot arc of your presence,
        all doubts will burn away.
        We will be ready to serve you with all our lives.
5 With heart and soul, with mind and strength, oh God, I believe;
        strip away all lingering doubts.
        We put our trust in you;
        you are our God.

PSALM 44:1–8
Does God take sides?

The original psalm sounds very like the football team that claims victory "because God was on our side." I have trouble with that theology.

1   The old folks talk about the good old days;
            they recall what God used to do, once upon a time.
2   **The bad guys lost, they say; the good guys always won.**
     God took vengeance upon tyrants, but set their victims free.
4, 3   **God took our side, they say.**
          We did not have the power or the money;
              we could not do it by ourselves.
                  If that's true,
          then God must have meddled in petty human quarrels.
5   **I have trouble believing that God takes sides.**

              In wars, even the winners lose.
     When a few abuse their privileges, everyone pays.
6   Our minds, our weapons, our technologies,
                  always turn against us.
              Money is a coward—
     it conspires to keep even repulsive dictators in power.
     Power corrupts, and absolute power corrupts absolutely.
7   **If we can be saved, it will be God's doing.**
          If we are saved, it will be in spite of ourselves.

8   **God does not take sides.**
              But God does save.
                  Thanks be to God.

PSALM 45:1–17
Advice for a new adventure

2   You are my dearest friend;
you are the brother I never had.
I trust you.
Your instincts are sound;
your life is above reproach.

3   So stand tall and step out confidently.
4   **You know what you stand for; you know what's right.**
Have the courage to take a stand;
defend your values vigorously.
5   Your words will penetrate to the heart of the issue;
your actions will expose the pretenses of your critics.

7   Because you refused to be swayed by opinion polls,
because you maintained your integrity,
you will find favor with both God and humans.

8   **But beware.**
9   The beautiful people and the media personalities
will compete to call themselves your friends.
10   **Do not be seduced by their charms;**
do not forget who you are.
11   People in high places will flatter you;
they will ask for your advice.
How can you resist?
12   The wealthy will want to shower you with gifts.
How can you refuse?
13   The camp followers will cling to you;
14 with perfect teeth and plastic virtue they will try to seduce you.
How can you ignore them?

15   Hold tight to your principles
when you enter the world of the rich and the famous,
the powerful and the ruthless.

16 **Keep your childlike innocence,
and all you meet will become your children;**
you will be a beloved grandfather to all.
17 **Then you will richly deserve your reputation,**
and people everywhere will recognize your wisdom.

PSALM 46
God says, "Stop it!"

1 Wars and rumors of wars swirl around us;
corporate conflicts engulf us.
Only God stands firm in these shifting sands.
God is our shelter from strife;
God gives us strength for the stresses of each day.
2 **We have nothing to fear.**
Though the social order is shaken,
though our leaders come crashing down,
3 though time-honored standards fly at half-mast
and the values we inherited are scorned—
even then, we have nothing to fear.

4 The comforting presence of God pours over us
like cool water on a burning beach;
it makes us glad.
5 God is with us;
God is an oasis of calm in a frenzy of feeding sharks.
The ambitious climb over each other;
the emperor stands naked in the clear eyes of innocence.
They are all frozen in their folly.
7 But God is with us; God is our sanctuary.

8 See how wonderfully the Lord works!
Those who would beat others have beaten themselves;
9 those obsessed with winning wind up as losers;
**those who think only of themselves
find that no one thinks of them at all.**
All their struggles add up to nothing.

10   **This is God's word to the warring: "Be still!**
Be still, and know that I—and only I—am God!"

11   **In the tumult of the nations,**
in the torment of the earth,
God is with us.
God is our sanctuary.
Thanks be to God.

PSALM 47:1–9
Give credit where it belongs

When an important person enters the room, we usually rise to our feet in respect.

1   Stand, please, in the presence of God.
2   **All other gods are pale imitations.**
     The Lord our God is one and only.

3   **God filled the earth with the energy we consume;**
God created the resources we depend on.
God taught us to harvest the fields and to tame the animals.
4   God charted our course for us,
from huddled huts in the woods
to elevators and airplanes.
5   **Under God's guidance, all creatures have evolved—**
from fruit fly to eagle, from penny whistle to symphony orchestra.
6   **Give the credit to God.**
7   As corporations give credit to the chief executive,
as governments give credit to the president or prime minister,
so all of us should give the credit to God.

8   **God sits at the head of the table.**
9   At God's table,
even the most powerful of people take lower places.
Give credit where it belongs.

PSALM 48
Above all other gods

Humans worship many things: power, status, pleasure, wealth, beauty... We worship them by devoting our time and attention to them. But these are all lesser gods.

1   When things go right, give God the praise;
    give God the glory.
2   Raise your eyes and see;
    the shadow of the Lord looms over us like a thundercloud.
3   Before that awesome might, no one risks defiance,
4   **not even the principalities and powers that rule this world.**
    They gather in force, confident of their powers;
5   **they disintegrate in chaos, aware of their weakness.**
6   The rain slices them into fragments.
    The hail drives them into the ground. They cry out in agony.
7   Like leaves before an autumn wind, they scatter.

8   **We do not lie;**
    we witness in truth to what we have seen and heard.
    The authority of God is above challenge;
    it surpasses all other gods that humans worship.

9   The reality of God is more than human minds can grasp;
    we can only struggle to understand.
10   The truth of God overwhelms our imaginations,
    despite our attempts to confine it to our comprehension.
11   **We know no more than to worship the Lord of creation,**
    the one who created us, and all creatures,
    and all communities of creatures.
    Let them all praise God.

12   Spend your life learning about this Lord,
13   **so that you may pass on to your successors the truth—**
14   that this is God.
    There is but one God, now and forever.
    This God will lead us forward into the future.

PSALM 49
The secret of success

A sage poses a riddle to the wheelers and dealers of this world.
This psalm makes no predictions about any kind of life after
death; it limits itself to this life.

1–3 Everyone wants to be rich.
Everyone imagines that money will solve all their problems.
Whether you're rich or poor, listen to these words!
4 I will unravel a riddle that has puzzled me for years.
5 **You know how it is when crises overcome you,**
when Murphy's Law entangles you in endless complications.
6 **Other people are doing fine,**
but for you everything is going wrong.
You worry.
You get jealous, angry, and fearful.
You struggle harder and harder.
7 **Why? Can you lift yourself off the ground**
by tugging at your shoelaces?
Can you buy wealth?
Can you gain the good life by killing yourself?

8 Your own efforts will never be enough.
9 **You may prolong your life a little, but you can't prevent death;**
10 you can reduce your taxes,
but you can't take wealth with you when you go.
11 **Even if you're worth more than some countries,**
you still occupy the same space in the ground when you die.
12 No matter what you are worth,
no matter what you have achieved,
you still come to the same end as an ant.

13 If you depend only on yourself in life,
you will have only yourself in death.
14 In the end, we are all equal;
ashes to ashes, dust to dust.

15 Only God transcends this endless cycle.
God is not mortal, nor limited by mortal things.
Only through God can anyone escape this mortal coil.
16 So what if you gain millions,
and have banks bowing and scraping?
17 **When you're gone, they'll bow and scrape to someone else.**
18 Pat yourself on the back for all your accomplishments,
but one thing you cannot accomplish—
you cannot live forever.
19 When you're gone, you're gone.
20 **Like a cow in a feeding stall,**
prosperity just makes you fatter when you go.
So don't worry about wealth.
In the end, it won't matter.

PSALM 50
The judge issues a warning

1 As an alarm drags us out of deep slumber,
2 so God rouses us from our lethargy.
3 **God does not sneak into our consciousness**
on soft-soled slippers.
God enters like a roaring lion,
a tornado rampaging across the prairie,
a parent who has already warned us three times.
4 **God cuts through our excuses.**
Feeble rationalizations cannot defend us.
5 **At baptism, at confirmation, at communion,**
we make promises.
God judges how we live up to our commitments.
6 **How can we challenge God's verdict?**
We know how often we have failed.

7 **God knows everything;**
God is the chief witness against us.
8 **"You have continually sacrificed yourself to other gods,"**
says God.

"You have chased after power and popularity,
after success and selfish pleasures."

9 **"Do not try to distract me with sweet words or generous
gifts," God warns.**
10 "Anything that you can offer me is already my own.
I made it.
I merely loaned it to you, to take care of.
11 I know every microbe by name;
I coiled the DNA in every cell.

12 "You can depend on nothing but my mercy," says God.
**"How can you buy your way out of your dilemma
when you have nothing to bribe me with?**
13 I don't eat steaks;
I don't drive luxurious cars;
I don't exploit immigrants and refugees as cheap labor.
14 **The only bribe you can offer me is a changed life.
That I will gladly accept.**
15 Start now," says God, "and I will save you.
Then you will be eternally grateful."

16 "Don't try to bargain with me!" God warns.
**"Don't prattle about good intentions,
about reading the Bible and going to church.**
Don't mouth your memorized confessions;
they will not convince me.
17 **You said the words, but you didn't live them.**
You didn't have the discipline to act on the truth you knew.
18 **You denounced thieves
but stole from others, calling it good business;**
you proclaimed the sanctity of the family
but lusted after lithe young bodies;
19 **you talked about honesty
while you spread lies about your competitors;**
20 you gossiped about your relatives;
you nursed grudges against your children.

21   Because I waited patiently for you to come to your senses,
you thought I didn't care.
But I do."

22   God passes sentence on us:
"You stand condemned by your own hypocrisy.
Now I will make an example of you."
23   **And God says to all, "If you have ears to hear, listen.**
Unless you want to share the same fate, smarten up.
Do not discredit God by your behavior;
in all your lives, make God visible for others."

PSALM 51:1–10
Ailing in body and spirit

Like Lady Macbeth, constantly trying to wash the blood off her hands, we feel a need to clean the stains off our lives.

1   Take pity on me, God.
As a god of love and of mercy, show mercy to me.
2   For I have disgraced myself, and you.
The stink of my sinning clings to my skin
like the spray of a skunk;
I cannot wash it off.
3   **I know too well what I have done;**
my past hangs over my future like a dark cloud.
4   **I took my chances, and cut my corners.**
I cared only what other people thought of me.
Now I see that each time I hurt another person, I hurt you.
You have every right to condemn me.
5   **But what else can you expect from me?**
I was conceived in a human womb, born to a human mother,
brought up in a human society.
6 **But you expect me to be holy like you, through and through.**
Teach me, then!
7   Scrape the crusted barnacles from my brain,
and fill it with fresh concepts;

**wipe my slate clean,
and give me new chalk to start again.**

9 If you must turn away from me, turn away from my bad side.
Close your eyes to my many weaknesses.
10   Give me a second chance, Lord;
start me over again, with a transplant of your holiness.

PSALM 51:1–12
Spring cleaning for the soul

*In spring, when our children were young, the frost coming out of
the ground turned our back yard into gooey mud. The children
came in filthy and half frozen. We popped them into a tub full of
hot water, and washed them pink and clean again.*

1   Scrub me clean, Lord.
Rub me down gently;
by your touch, show how much you love me;
flush away my failures;
2 sponge off the stains of constant compromise;
help me clean up my act.

3   You don't have to tell me—
I know too well what I have been doing.
4   **I know I have let you down;**
I have betrayed your trust in me.
You warned me;
you have every right to be angry.
Don't blame yourself because I blew it;
5   I was born this way.
How can I help it? I'm only human.
6 So wash out my mind, and rinse out my heart.
New life starts on the inside, with knowing myself.
7 Scrub my spirit clean, and swirl my soiled nature down the drain;
let me step out fresh and sparkling.
8   Mend my fractured spirits.

9 **Turn a blind eye to my faults,**
and cherish the scars where I have fallen down.

10 **A fresh start begins with a pure heart, oh God,**
so let me share your spirit.
11 I do not want to be cut off from you;
I do not want to live without you.
12 Take me back into your good graces.
Help me, Lord, for I really want to please you.

PSALM 51:10–17
Seeking a cure

*You can't pass a magazine rack or a bookstand without seeing
something about a diet or a disease, a new crisis or a new cure.
If only we took our spiritual health as seriously.*

10b Let your spirit circulate freely within me, God.
11 **I can no more live without your spirit**
than I can live without my own blood.
10a Clean the cholesterol out of my arteries.
12 Help me with a transfusion of your holiness;
restore my life.

13 Then I will stand straight and walk bravely.
Then the skeptics will have to eat their words;
then they will have to believe in you.
14 **Keep me from arguing with them, God,**
but let me sing your praises in every beat of my heart.
15 **Give me courage to speak of you, especially to those who scoff.**

16 **What do you want of me?**
You won't be satisfied with token gifts;
charitable donations will not buy you off.
17 Only the end of self-centered egotism is enough;
When I purge my selfish thoughts,
you will welcome me home.

PSALM 51:1–17
Hormones rampant

An acquaintance calls his teenaged son "the walking hormone."
Little wonder, for our society has made sexual attraction a
cultural obsession.

1   Sometimes I hate myself, God.
I talk with a woman, and all I can think about is her body.
I meet a man, and all I can see is his looks.
2   **Can't you get my mind off sex?**
3   You know what's going on inside my skull.
4   **Even if I haven't actually sinned against another person,**
I have sinned against you.
You teach me that every person matters in your sight;
to you, age and sex and appearance make no difference.
5   When I see people as objects, as toys for my own gratification,
I deny your unconditional love.
6   **You want me to be honest with you, God.**
Now I'm being honest.
Don't condemn me for it.
7, 10   **Help me clean up my mind, God.**
Help me clean up my act.
8   Help me relate to others with no hidden agendas.
Broken bones grow stronger when they mend;
heal my broken relationships.
9   Overlook my obsessions;
do not hold my failings against me.

10   **Straighten out the warped logic**
of the excuses I make for myself.
14   Do not let my lusts govern me.
11   **Do not reject me;**
without you, I am blown around by every puff of peer pressure.
12   **Make me what I was meant to be,**
when you first thought of me.
13   When others see the change in me,
perhaps they too will pay attention to you.

15   **When my actions match my thoughts,**
       when my thoughts match my beliefs,
       then I can witness to others with integrity.
16   My own efforts accomplish no more
       than beating my head against a brick wall.
17   **What matters is a genuine change of heart.**
       You will value that more than buckets of broken promises.

PSALM 52:1–9
Moral bankruptcy

A dissenter thumbs her nose at the powerful.

1   You boast about beating your competitors;
       you brag about evading taxes;
       you use other people's money for leveraged financing.
2   **You think you're worth millions.**
       But everything you do exposes your moral bankruptcy.
3   **You'd rather lord it over your neighbors than love them;**
       you'd rather knife your employees than nurture them.
4   **You're a bundle of malevolent reflexes.**
5   Someday, you will get what you deserve.
       Your spouse will leave you,
       your children will despise you,
       your colleagues will avoid you.
    Your empires will come crashing down around your shattered ego.
6   **Even those you exploited will laugh at you.**
7   They'll say, "How the mighty are fallen!"
    They'll laugh, "The bigger you are, the harder you fall!"

8   I'm not powerful or successful.
       I'm a child compared to you.
    But I ride my roller coasters in the park, not in the stock market.
       I'd rather hold a hand than a meeting.
9   What I do, I do for God.
       If any credit is due, I give it to God.
    And God frees me to enjoy the goodness of living.

PSALM 53
A fable

It seemed to me futile to attempt to put the case any more plainly than the psalm itself does. So I looked for an analogy. If God were a cat, would humans act like rats?

1 Rats tell themselves, "There is no cat."
They skulk in the walls;
they feast on carrion, and belch.
You can't trust a rat.
2 The cat crouches by the hole and waits;
the cat watches to see if any rats will change their nature.
3 But rats will be rats.
There's no such thing as a good rat.
4 **If they were ignorant, they could be forgiven.**
But this is their way.
They prey on the sick, the weak, the helpless.
They deny the dominance of cats.
5 **So they live in constant terror.**
They hide in walls and sewers
because they dare not come out into the light.
They are creatures of the dark.
6 They know that if they risk the daylight, like any honest rodent,
a mighty paw will strike them;
sharpened claws will slash them,
and the streets will be safer.
Then a great shout of joy will echo within the walls,
and all creatures will be glad.

PSALM 54
Winning friends back

1 I don't know what to do, Lord;
I don't know where to turn.
2 I need you, God.
Listen to my plight.

74   **James Taylor**

3   I would turn to my colleagues, my friends, my spouse.
But they have turned against me.
They leap to conclusions;
they judge me without hearing my defense.

4   **You are my only hope, God.**

5   Show them how wrong they have been;
make them see the error of their ways.

6   I would not try to bribe you—
but get me out of this,
and I will be your loyal friend for ever.

7   **I don't want to have enemies, God.**
I want them to be friends again.
The only triumph over enemies is to turn them into friends.

PSALM 57
From rejection to rejoicing

1   Take pity on me, oh God! Have pity on me!
I have no one else to turn to.
The storms of life buffet me;
I huddle in the shelter of your strength.

2   Do not dump me out into the deluge
clinging to tiny twigs for comfort.
Only you are strong enough to bear the brunt of the storm.

3   Carrying crosses is your destiny;
for this you came into being,
to deflect the demonic things that drive me into despair.
Send me sunshine and warm breezes for a change,
and let me feel wrapped in summer for a while.

4   My feet are frozen in a block of ice.
The cold burns its way up my legs.
I cannot stand it, but I cannot move.

5   Only you, oh God, are above all this agony and anguish.
From the heavens, you see the earth enveloped in glory.

6   My enemies tried to trap me.
They wove a web of lies to entangle me.

With my head hanging down, I could not see it.
But they got mired in their own mess;
their downfall showed me my own danger.

7 **And so my heart can sing like an uncaged lark.**
I am no longer a prisoner;
I have been set free!

8 **Sing, my soul, sing to the skies!**
Let all the world join my song,
join the chorale of praise for a new day.

9 **Even if I sing alone, I must praise you, oh Lord;**
I will sing your praises among all creatures;
all nations and all peoples shall hear it.

10 If I could cover the sky with song,
I would not begin to reveal your wonder;
your love fills the universe as the oceans fill the seas.

11 You, oh God, are above all our agony and anguish.
From the heavens, you see the earth enveloped in glory.

PSALM 62:5–12
A bad morning

*Sometimes you just want to tell everyone to go away and leave
you alone. The feeling may not be rational, but it's real.*

5 I don't want to see anyone.
I want to stay in bed and pull the blankets up over my head.

6 People are unfaithful two-faced phonies.
I don't want them.
I just want God with me.

7 I can't trust anyone else, any more.
No one has any honor, any loyalty.

8 The only one I can trust is God.

9 **People today have no standards, no enduring values.**
They flit from fad to fad like butterflies.
The upper crust are all sham and show;
the highly educated are windbags, inflating their egos.

A breeze could blow them all away.
10 It's not worth trying to beat them at their own game.
Don't stoop to their methods.
You'll only drag yourself down to their level.
11 Do things God's way, instead.
12 **God doesn't compete, and God doesn't seek revenge.**
God simply loves.
**That's all that God expects of you,
and of me, too.**

Now I feel better.
I can get up now and start the day.

PSALM 63:1–8
Holy presence

*Why do we need downtown churches? Because a few people still
come there to seek sanctuary.*

1 Endless crowds of people crush me.
They jostle my mind; they crack my concentration.
I feel like no more than a means to an end, a cog in the machinery.
I long for the gentle touch of loving fingers,
the intimate whisper of acceptance.
2 **So I come looking for you, Lord, in your holy places.**
3 In this dimmed light, in this hushed silence,
I sense your presence.
4 **I wish I could feel you as near me
in the rabid frenzy of life in the city core.**
I want to reach out and touch you
in the marketplace as well as the chancel.
5 **Then I will not feel alone;**
you will be part of every thought and every breath.
6 **I will know you at my desk and in my den,**
in my bed and in my bathtub.
7 **Nothing will come between us.**
8 And I will hold you close in the nighttime of my fears.

PSALM 65:1–13
Thanksgiving

1   We can't put it off any longer, God.
2   **We come crawling to you,**
because we have all fallen short of your expectations.
3   We have all missed the mark.
But you have not held our failures against us.
5   We stumbled, and you picked us up;
we were sinking, and you helped us swim.
4   You treat us with honor and respect.
You make us welcome.
It is more than we dare ask, more than we could ever expect.

6   **We have no right to such kindness.**
You are the creator of the world.
You push mountains into ranges;
you calm the raging oceans;
·7   **you spin the earth on its axis.**
Before you, we are as insignificant as ants,
parading our puny armies.
8   **If you stamp your feet, we will be squashed.**

9   We boast of our science and technology,
but by ourselves we cannot make a single seed sprout;
we cannot shape a single raindrop.
10   We destroy, but only you bring life.
11 **Through the cycle of the seasons, with reckless generosity,**
you share the wealth of the earth.
12   As tiny drops of dew gather into rushing streams,
so our small thoughts gather into a gush of gratitude.
13   **The whole world celebrates your goodness.**
Like dolphins dancing through the waves,
like antelope prancing through long grass,
the whole earth leaps in exuberant gratitude.

PSALM 66:1–9
The promised land

*A song of immigrants and settlers and refugees, and of anyone
recovering from serious illness or debility.*

1 On the far side of the mountains, a new world spreads before us.
2 **Rocky ridges give way to rolling grasslands;**
  the shadows of our past give way to endless sunshine.
4 **The far horizon shimmers in holy celebration.**
  In sacred silence we stand,
  speechless before the rebirth of possibility.

3 **You tested us terribly, God.**
  At times, we thought we would die, adrift, alone.
5 **You scorched us on the deserts;**
  you froze us on the glaciers.
  We could not help ourselves.
6 But you gave us shade against the sun,
  and fire against the cold.
  With your help, we survived every obstacle.
7 Through our trials you taught us
  that you alone are almighty, and not we ourselves.

8 **We owe our survival to God.**
  We had run out of our own resources.
9 **But God kept us alive and struggling;**
  God kept us on our feet when no one else cared.

PSALM 66:10–20
People with a purpose

Trauma and tragedy seem to destroy some people but to strengthen others.

10 We have been rejected and despised,
persecuted and punished.
But we have come out of our ordeal stronger.
11 Once, we were simply a flood of frightened individuals.
We had nothing in common but fear.
Now we have become a people with a purpose;
our trials have unified us.
12 We were the eternal victims;
we were captives and oppressed.
Yet God brought us through to this new world.
13 **We will repay God for keeping watch over us.**
From now on, the best of everything we have belongs to God.
14 **We made that promise when we were desperate;**
we will keep our promise when we are well off.
15 Without God, we would have nothing.
16 **So we will tell our children,**
and they will tell their children,
what God has done for us.

17 **We were lost and lonely,**
a wandering people, unsure of our future.
And God responded to our plight.
18 God was not like diplomats and immigration officials;
God did not judge us by our appearance
or our bank accounts.
20 Even during the toughest of our trials,
we never felt that God had abandoned us.
Thanks be to God.

PSALM 67
Gratefulness

1   God is good to us, God treats us right;
      night and day, God smiles on us.
2   God has chosen us,
         God has made us a mirror
   to show the world the nature of God's personality.
3   **Let the people praise you, Lord;**
         let all the people praise you.

4   Every country on every continent can be grateful to you.
      Every people and every race can see how just you are.
5   **Let the people praise you, Lord;**
         let all the people praise you.

6   The good earth feeds us, fruit and vine;
            God trusts us to take care of it.
7   Every field and every forest lifts its produce toward heaven.
         Let the people praise you, Lord;
         let all the people praise you.

PSALM 67
The garden of earth

1   Send us mild temperatures and gentle breezes, God;
   make your sun shine softly and your rain fall regularly.
      Then we will know that you smile upon us, and bless us.
2 **Then all will recognize your kindness, your power to save.**
3   And the people will praise you, God.
            All the people will praise you.

4   **The nations will know you are not capricious.**
            You do not favor one over another.
   You do not give rain to one and drought to another;
      you do not feed one and starve another.

6 **The earth pours out its produce without stinting;**
  like our God, it withholds nothing.
7 **Who then are we to withhold anything from others?**
  As God has blessed us, let us bless others.
5 **Then indeed will all the peoples praise you, God;**
  all nations will know you and praise you.

PSALM 68:5–10, 32–35
Flowers in God's garden

5 In God's generous creation,
  no one needs to be an orphan or an outcast.
6 **Every thing has its proper place;**
  our lives are linked in endless ways.
  Only those who consider themselves equal with God
  will find themselves out on their own.

7 But we are not alone.
  Not in the pounding fear of race riots,
  not in the humiliation of soup kitchens,
  not in the panic of emergency wards.
  God has been with us.
8 **We still got wet when it rained;**
  we still got muddy when we fell—
  God didn't protect us from pain.
9 But the rain brought out the flowers;
  the mud enriched the earth;
10 And God turned our wintry wilderness
  into a meadow of milk and honey.

32 **As flowers in God's garden,**
  we lift our bright and varied faces to the holy one.
33 Our colors reflect the rainbow,
  the colors that God flings across the heavens.
34 **Who among humans can make a seed sprout,**
  a flower form, a tree bear fruit?

35 God hovers over the earth,
giving life and strength to all creation.
Give the glory to God.

PSALM 69:7–18
The burden of imperfection

A young man with cerebral palsy told me why he once tried to commit suicide.

7 I'm tired of being treated with contempt.
I can't stand people completing sentences for me.
I don't want to be different.
8 **Nobody knows what it's like—**
not even my sister or my parents.
9 I've tried, God.
I've tried to ignore the snickers, the ridicule.
I've tried not to mind
always being the last one picked for a team.
They look away when I drool;
they insist on helping me when I don't need it.
Companies and organizations use me.
They put me on display
to show that they hire the handicapped.
11 I've played along.
12 But it hasn't changed anything.
I'm still the outsider, the incompetent, the laughingstock.

13 Can you understand what it's like, God?
Can you, in your perfection, know what it's like
to be imperfect?
Can you love me in spite of my handicaps?
14 **Sometimes suicide seems the only way out.**
I tried it once.
15 But I was too scared.
All I could see ahead was a black hole, a bottomless pit.
I couldn't face my fear of nothingness.

16 Now I hang between that nothingness
and the emptiness of my life.
Pull me back from the brink, Lord.
17 **Don't you reject me too.**
18 Hold my hand. Draw me back to life.
Set me free from the prison of my faulty body.

PSALM 70
A voice from the bottom

*It hurts to be just a little bit slower, a little less street-smart, a
little less competent, than others.*

1 You can do it if you want to, God—
you can end my humiliation.
2 **There are people who want to shame me;**
they make everything so confusing.
3 **When I make mistakes, they shake their heads.**
They say, "I told you so."

4 **God, you promised us.**
"Come unto me, all who are weary and heavy laden," you said,
"and I will give you rest."
5 **I am poor and heavy laden, God.**
Give me rest. Give me peace. Give me justice.
I am too tired to wait forever, God.
Do it now!

PSALM 71:1-6
Rescue from the bullies

Some translations call this "an old man's prayer" (because of verse 9) but I chose to paraphrase this part from a child's viewpoint. Every one of us has been a child; only a few have been old—yet.

1   Don't let them make fun of me.
Let me hide myself behind your skirts.
2   Comfort me and protect me;
listen to my fears, and enfold me in your arms.
3   When I am in trouble, I run to you.
I have no one but you to rely on.
4   The big kids won't leave me alone;
their hands reach out and grab at me.
Rescue me from their clutches.

5   From the time I was tiny, you have been my refuge.
I have always been able to trust you.
6   Before I was born, I felt safe in your womb.
As an infant, I rested on your breast.
You are all I have, and all I ever had.

PSALM 71:7-14
Relief from too long a life

7a   People stare at me. They see the creases in my face;
they open doors for me, and catch me when I stumble.
They pity me.
9   **Don't despise me too, God,**
when my mind fails and my muscles weaken.
Most of my friends and relatives have died already;
my children have moved away—
don't you abandon me too!
12   **Don't be distant from me, oh my God;**
don't leave me alone in my rented room.
10   **I have no one close any more;**

everyone is a stranger.
11 **They pity me.**
13 Someday they'll know what it's like;
old age will catch up with them, too.
Then they'll understand—
they will regret their former attitudes.
14 **As my body fails, I hang all my hope on you.**
I look forward with longing to joining you.
7b **You are my rock, the unchanging element of my life.**
8 I will concentrate on you, every day I have left.

PSALM 72:1–7, 10–14
If powerful people played fair

Politicians get caught playing hanky-panky. Business leaders make bad investments, that we have to bail out for billions of dollars. These people outrage us, because they failed to follow the standards they expect of us.

1 If only powerful people could be more like you, God.
2 **They would apply the same standards to their own lives**
that they demand of those who depend on them.
3 Then employees might enjoy working;
press releases would tell the truth;
industrial dumps would not defile the world.
4 **Powerful people would selflessly serve their constituencies;**
they would not exploit for short-term profit
those who have less money, less power, and less influence.
5 **Such people would earn our long-term loyalty;**
they would deserve to prosper.
7 **Their radical example would make others**
reconsider their own attitudes.

10 All the world would recognize this remarkable approach;
11 **all the world would come to see how it is done.**
12 Amazing—people in positions of power
who do not manipulate events for their own benefit!

86   **James Taylor**

They do what they do for the least of their customers;
13 they treat single mothers, natives, immigrants, and teenagers
    as people of worth, not merely as potential consumers.
14   **For them there are no mass markets;**
            every individual is precious as a person.
6   **We need that kind of leadership.**

PSALM 72:1–8
Good and Godly leadership

*From this psalm (verse 8), came the original motto of the new
nation of Canada: God shall have "dominion from sea to sea."*

1   Let every leader be as just as you, oh God.
2   **Let every leader judge the poor properly;**
           the poor need justice even more than the rich.
3   **Even when prosperity piles up like mountains,
           let it not bury those who need fair treatment most.**
4   Wise leaders will watch out for the weak;
           they will protect the poor from the greedy;
           they will keep would-be tyrants on a tight leash.
5   **As long as the grass grows and the rivers run,
           let God be our model.**
6   God's justice is as welcome as rain on parched prairie,
           as sunshine after a long winter.
7   It causes peace and harmony to blossom in arid soil;
           friendship flowers in God's footprints.
8   Then indeed will God reign supreme from sea to sea,
           from the headwaters to the mouths of the rivers.

PSALM 72:1–7, 10–14
A lullaby of hope

1   Life will be different for you, my child.
2   **You will break out of our prisons of oppression,
           our ghettos of injustice.**

3 Your mountains will rise clear in the morning.
Your valleys will offer cozy comfort in the setting sun.
4 You will not fall prey to prevailing values;
you will never exploit the powerless,
or profit from people's desperation.
5 **Adversity will not grind you down,**
6 nor will difficulties dissolve your determination.
They will only help you grow.
7 A bubble of peace will protect you;
10 **a sea of calm will support you.**
They will all see it in you, my child;
everyone will see it.
12, 14 You will do better than us.
You will not be bowed down by despair, nor bent by hate.
You will not be crushed by violence;
you will not grovel for power.
13 You will be free to love, to care, to have compassion.
14 **You are precious, my child.**
For you, things will be different.

PSALM 73:1–24
The rich and the famous

*Old Testament professor and guru Walter Brueggemann
considers this a favorite psalm.*

1 God works in mysterious ways.
I believed that God looks after the good, the salt of the earth.
Their hearts are pure, their behavior fair.
2 **But I had my doubts.**
3 For I saw who made it onto the talk shows,
and who got elected,
and who won the grand prize in the lotteries.
The bigger the mouth, the more arrogant the opinion,
the more likely they are to get ahead.
4 Fortune favors them.
They look gorgeous.

88 James Taylor

5   **They shrug off troubles, like water off a duck's back.**
6   They wear pride like their sharkskin suits and coiffed hair;
     they don't care who they stand on to climb to the top.
7   Their eyes bug out with ambition;
     their mouths ooze sincerity.
8   **They consider themselves above criticism;**
     they resort to the courts the way alcoholics turn to booze.
9   **They claim to believe in God,**
     but every gesture makes them liars.
10   Yet people idolize them;
     wherever they go, people want a handshake or an autograph.
12   And the money keeps rolling in.

13   **Why then have I bothered to be good?**
     Why have I kept God's commandments?
14   **All day, I labor at minimum wage;**
     I have no time or money for anything more than necessities.
16   **There just doesn't seem to be any justice.**

17   Then I read the scriptures and study the psalms.
18   I suspect that God set them for a fall—
19   **like a balloon, the bigger they are,**
     the louder they pop.
     It takes only one night's indiscretion, one unguarded word
     and they are gone.
     The sharks circle in for the kill;
     the mass media tear them to shreds.
20   They are no more than a bad dream,
     a fading memory in the morning's light.
21   **Now I'm sorry I felt bitter.**
     Now I regret my anger.
22   **I was stupid and ignorant, God.**
     I should have trusted you.
24   **From now on, I will try to recognize your wisdom.**
     Please forgive me, and take me back into your circle of friends.

PSALM 76
God never gives up

A mediator must never give up, never quit trying, never fall asleep.

1   God is real.
God has a name and an address:
2   **God lives here, in this place, among us.**
3   Day by day, the mystery of God's presence peeks through
in unexpected little miracles
like children skipping in playgrounds,
swallows swooping under clear skies,
ice cream trucks in the desert,
and receptionists who remember your name.

4   You, God, are more eternal than the most ancient rocks,
more present than the air we breathe.
5   **Weapons of war rust and wear out;**
the latest technology grows obsolete.
6   In time, battles and campaigns all become boring;
pillaging and looting lose their appeal.
We weary of perpetual conflict.
7   **But you never give up, God.**
Never-ending negotiation does not wear you out.
8   **You know how things ought to be;**
you keep provoking us with your persistent vision.
9   You sort through the rubble of human discord,
seeking tiny pearls of harmony.
You polish them, and hold them up for all to see.
10   No wonder people praise you for your integrity,
your consistency, your persistence.

11   **You can depend on God.**
So make your commitments,
confident that you will be able to fulfill them.
Put your promises into action;
make sacrifices to prove you mean what you say.

12   **For God will not tolerate hypocrisy;**
        if you don't mean what you say,
        no power on earth can protect you.

PSALM 77:1–2, 11–20
A doubter's affirmation

1   Like an infant isolated by its incubator, I wail.
        But no one responds.
2   Like a worker laid off after 30 years of loyal service,
        I roam the streets restlessly.
        But no one responds.
11   Still, I will not give up hope;
12   **Even if you are not around, I remember you.**

13   You did not give up when we let you down.
14,15 **You opened the mysteries of nature to provide for our needs.**
16   When we needed metal, you taught us to mine.
    When we needed irrigation, you supplied lakes and rivers.
        When we needed energy, you led us to oil.
19   **We took the credit;**
        we told ourselves it was all our own doing.
        And we fouled your world with our wastes.
17   **But your winds still wipe the grime from our skies;**
18   your rains still renew our fields;
        your seas still sustain our climate.
20   How then can I doubt you?

PSALM 78:1–7
Women's wisdom

In prehistoric times, I imagine, much knowledge was passed down as women gathered around the campfire to do their daily chores.

1 Come, children, and sit beside me.
Listen while I tell you a story.
2 I will teach you the wisdom of many generations
3 distilled into deceptively simple sayings.
We women have not roamed the world as solitary hunters;
ours has been the hearth and the home,
nurturing the lives of our loved ones.
4 **In endless talk of nothing much,**
we learn from each other's trials and troubles.
We pass our collective wisdom along as aphorisms:
A stitch in time... A rolling stone...
Sleeping dogs... Glass houses...
Each maxim gleams with its own gem of truth,
sifted from the sands of time.
5 **Through our collective consciousness, God guides us.**
Individual insights melt into communal memory.
6 **That is how we pass our hard-won wisdom on**
to generations not yet conceived.

Someday, children, you will tell your grandchildren,
7 **So that they too can know**
that they belong to the people of God,
so that they too can be a light to the nations,
a path pointing the way toward God.

James Taylor

PSALM 78:1–7
Tell me a story: 1

*We all need family histories. No one is so poor as the person
with no roots.*

1   If I say, "Once upon a time,"
everyone knows a story is starting.
2   I do not know the meanings of my stories;
I merely pass them on as they were passed to me.
3   Only you can decide what they mean to you.

4   **This is our story. This is where we came from.**
When you hear this story, you must also tell it,
so that others may also know where they came from.
5   **Our story is not limited to our own lives.**
We belong to a long line of travelers,
snaking in single file through history;
**we bear with us the beliefs
the convictions, the experiences
bequeathed to us
by those who passed this way before.**
From Abraham and Sarah, from Rachel and Jacob,
from David and Bathsheba, from Mary and Jesus,
we learn our family story.
6   **Only by knowing where we have come from
can we know where we are going.**
7   Only by knowing who we are
can we know that God is with us.

PSALM 78:12–16
Tell me a story: 2

Remember that this partial psalm does not stand alone; it needs to be read in connection with the sections before and after.

12 **Once upon a time, we were slaves.**
We were exploited for economic growth,
and held captive by capital.
13 **But God freed us from the prisons of our past.**
God flung open our minds, and let us see new possibilities.
14 **By signs and symbols, God led us to new life.**
15 In arid canyons of crisis,
God showed us how to drink deeply of life.
16 **In barren wastelands of despair, God gave us hope.**

PSALM 78:23–29
Tell me a story: 3

23 When we were starving for affection, God found us friends.
24 **Their cupboards fed us;**
we gained courage from their company.
25 We could not have asked for more.

26 **When we were mired in our own misery,**
God set our feet on firm ground.
When self-defeating thoughts entangled us,
God dusted the cobwebs from our minds.
When we were frozen with fears,
God warmed us in loving arms.
27 Like northern marshes opening icy ponds to the summer sun,
we respond to God's goodness.
God has restored us to life.

29 **Once we were slaves, but God set us free.**
28 Freedom is an attitude; we can take it with us, wherever we go. ·
29 **What more could we ask?**

PSALM 78:34–38
Moments of truth

*We all have our moments of truth, when our lives flash before
our eyes...*

34   You stand paralyzed in front of a skidding car.
         You slip on an icy sidewalk.
         Your supervisor hauls you on the carpet.
         And a miracle happens.
         You aren't hit; you don't fall; you aren't fired.
35   **You want to thank God.**
36   **But you don't know how, any more.**
         You've spent too long muttering empty words
         and making empty promises.
37   **You didn't mean what you said;**
         you didn't do what God wanted.
38   **God has more than enough reason to reject you.**
         If God wanted, you could fall through nothingness forever.
         But God loves you.
         And so God listens.
     And God hears the thanks you don't know how to say.

PSALM 79:1–9
Vandalism

For all victims of senseless violence.

1   They didn't have to do this, God.
         The broken glass, the spray paint,
         the upholstery slashed, the tables turned upside down.
2   **They even killed the canary.**
         Do they call this fun?
3   **They dumped the contents of the cabinets on the floor,**
         and flung our precious books against the walls.
         There is no way we can clean up this mess.

4　　Do they really hate us this much?
What did we do to offend them?
5　　If they need someone to vent their anger on,
why not dump on those who deserve it?
6　　Let them lash out at economic systems
that protect bank accounts and penalize jobs;
at competition that grabs from the weak
and gives to the strong;
at governments who sell their countries
to balance their budgets.
8　　Vandals claim they're settling old scores,
responding to old injustices.
How can they hold us accountable
for the attitudes of our grandparents?
9　　Merciful God, give us the courage to carry on.

PSALM 80:1–7, 17–19
Springtime of the soul

Northerners have a special perception of winter.

1　　As a tulip bulb buried beneath the earth
senses the warmth of spring,
as a lilac bud swells with sap, ready to burst into leaf,
2　　so your people wait for your coming.
Do not delay, we beg you.
3　　Thaw our frozen hearts;
give us courage to risk sending out new shoots.
4　　Don't keep us closed in endless winter.
5　　We have been locked too long in lifeless night.
6　　No one believes there is life left in us.
7　　Send some summer into our lives, God.
We wait for you.

17　　Let the sun warm the earth again,
so that our stems can grow tall and straight,
and our blossoms lift their faces to the sky.

18   **Take away this winter of our discontent,**
    and we will not let you down.
    Give us life, and we will give you glory.
19   **Send spring quickly, oh creator.**
    Let your garden grow again!

PSALM 80:1–7, 17–19
The view from outside

At Christmas, the ostentatious flaunting of wealth and family must be very painful for those who have neither.

1   Can't you hear us knocking on your door?
    You stand inside, laughing in the firelight with your family;
    you toy with your tinsel and your ornaments.
    Can't you hear us?
2   We are the lost and the lonely, out in the cold.
3   **We long for something to celebrate too.**
4   How long can you ignore us?
    How long can you close your eyes and ears to our crisis?
5   Hunger gnaws on our bones;
    we sip the salt of our tears.
6   We are an embarrassment.
    People turn away from us.
    They laugh and joke; they don't even see us.
    We are invisible.
7   **Let us live too. Please, let us live.**

17   We have nothing with which to thank you.
    But God will reward you in ways you cannot imagine.
    God will heal your former blindness;
    you will touch a world you have never imagined.
18   You will not want to return to your old ways.
    Respond to our pleas, and see for yourself.
19   **Let us live too. Please, let us live.**

PSALM 80:8-18
The gardener goes away

8 You grew this garden yourself, God.
You tilled the soil, and pulled the weeds.
9 You planted the seeds and watered it.
10 **It became a place of beauty.**
The sweet scent of lilacs filled the air;
11 **blue lupins stood tall,**
and shy pansies turned bright faces to the sun.

12 Why did you stop caring, God?
13 **Kids from the playground trample your tulips;**
commuters use it as a shortcut;
dogs dig up your flower beds.
16 Fires smolder in heaps of windblown refuse,
and seedlings wilt for lack of water.

·14 Come back, God.
Come back and take care of us again.
15 Restore your garden to its rightful glory.
17 **Take control over this chaos,**
18 and we will gladly live under your green thumb forever.

PSALM 81
Graduation day

A parent celebrates a child's graduation.

1 My heart is so full, I cannot make a sound.
2 But surely the air shimmers with excitement;
the lights glow brighter;
the dust disappears from the corners
of this vast and musty auditorium.
3, 4 **This is our special day, the day we have waited for so long.**
7 All these years we have struggled. We have made payments.
We skimped and scrounged, we pushed and prodded.

5, 6   **And now it is done!**
       We have succeeded!
       We have reached our goal;
       life will never be the same.

And God asks some difficult questions.

8   In your celebration, where is there room for me?
     In your joy, what credit do you give to me?
9   You have made your goal an idol;
     you have let it take over your lives.
10   I am the one who has watched over you.
I am the one who sustained you through the tough times.
     I fed you and nurtured you and kept you going.
       I am the one; I am God.

11   You were obsessed by your own concerns.
12   So I left you alone, to do it your way.
       I did not interfere.
13 If only you had paid as much attention to me as to your goals,
14   I would have given you many more times to rejoice
                 along the way.
15   **It would have been much less of a struggle.**
16   This moment would be just as sweet,
     with no trace of bitterness or regret.

PSALM 82
Tough love

It's nice to think of a loving God. But love does not render God toothless.

1   God sits at the head of the table.
2   **"How long," God demands,**
     "will you keep making the wrong choices?
     How long will your policies favor injustice?

3   **I expect you to be fair to everyone,**
    including those with no economic weight;
    to defend the rights of those who have no voice,
    and no one to speak for them;
4   **to protect the weak and the struggling from exploitation.**
5   Of all people, they need your protection most.
    They do not have education, or money,
    or friends in high places.
    They have suffered devastating losses in their lives."

6   **God says: "You think you have taken over my responsibilities.**
7   **But you are not God.**
    When your time comes,
    you will die like everyone else."

8   **Come, Lord.**
    Come judge the earth.
    We are yours to judge.

PSALM 84:1–7
In praise of gardeners

Originally, this psalm praised the Temple in Jerusalem. We now believe the whole earth is God's temple.

1   What a gorgeous home you have, God.
    Its beauty takes my breath away.
2   **My heart longs to live here in harmony with your wishes.**

3   In your home, nothing is too small to matter.
    Every butterfly has its blossom;
    every groundhog has its burrow;
    every river has its valley.
4   The separate songs of every entity well up as one,
    blending their voices in harmony.
5   **Some blindly obey their instincts;**
    others derive their inspiration directly from you.

6   **Even when they go through hell,**
           they transform it into a garden;
           green grows from the touch of their thumbs.
7   Their love of life grows stronger and stronger,
           for they see you in everything.

PSALM 84
A passionate lover

We rarely think of the psalms as love poems—but how else can you describe the feeling of this psalm?

1   I love you, God.
2   **My heart races when I am in your presence;**
           my blood pulses with joy when I think of you.

3   **You never turn anything away from you.**
           You encourage swallows to nest under your eaves
           and worms to tunnel in your earth.
4   **Each creature plays its part in your universal symphony.**

5   Whatever strength we have, we get from you.
           Refreshed and renewed, we rise eager for each new day,
           and find that every road leads us to you.
6   In apartment blocks and office towers,
      high-rise filing cabinets filled with despair, you comfort us;
           When narrow minds turn into cold shoulders,
           you renew us.
7   When we cannot cope, you carry us.
9   **You see us, you know us, you look into our hearts.**
           You lift us up when our knees melt with weariness;
8   **You hear our prayers.**

       You stand beside us, even when we cannot recognize you.
           So we call on you, oh God of Gods.
       Creator of the universe, hear the plea of your creation.
10   **Take me as your lover.**

I would rather be dirt swept before your broom
than a polished brass plaque in anyone else's boardroom.
An hour in your company is more stimulating
than a day at Disneyland.
11　　You are like the sun that burns away the morning fog;
you are as fresh as the air after a spring shower;
deceit and deception have no part in your personality.

12　　　　**You are the kind of God I want to live with.**

PSALM 85:1–2, 8–13
An unfair world

A friend got AIDS from a blood transfusion. It doesn't seem fair.
Job's comforters still offer the wrong responses.

1　　　　Pious voices utter platitudes:
·"Trust in the Lord. It's God's will. God knows best."
2　　　　People say with certainty:
"The Lord gives, and the Lord taketh away."
"With faith, all things are possible."

8　　　　"Silence!" I want to shout.
"Take your frozen formulas and leave me alone!
Let me listen for what God has to say.

9　**For God will not let a broken heart bleed by itself in the night.**
10　　　　When wounds cut to the bone,
only God can sew together the torn edges of a shattered life.
Only God can soothe such throbbing pain."

11　　　Surely goodness and mercy will grow again,
and sunshine return to the sky.
12　　　　Sorrow is holy ground;
walk on it only with feet bared to the pain of every pebble.
13　　　Through the storm, the Lord of life
comes walking on the salt sea of tears.

PSALM 85:1–9
Forgiven

How should we act, when a young man or woman, an adult but still a child, dishonors our reputation? Again and again. And what should God do, when our actions damage God's reputation?

1 　　　　You have forgiven us before.
2 　　**When we made mistakes, you took us back.**
3 　　　You were angry, but you didn't take it out on us;
　　you were upset, but you didn't nurse a grudge.
4 　　　　　Do it again, God.
　　Forgive us; we didn't know what we were doing.
5 　　　Don't hold our faults against us forever—
　　forever is a long long time.
6, 7 　　　　We were not ourselves;
　　we cannot be ourselves when we are cut off from you.
　　　Take us back into your good graces,
　　　　and let us laugh and sing again.

8 　　**We admit we have done wrong.**
　　　We have hurt you. We're sorry.
9 　**Tell us what we need to do, to earn your love again.**

PSALM 86:1–10, 16–17
The hope of the hopeless

Feel free to substitute your own specific references for the people and places mentioned in this paraphrase.

1 　　　　Please, God, listen to me.
　　I am a single mother on welfare.
　　　I am a native boy on the reserve.
　　I am a refugee.
2 　　　I have tried to follow your ways, God.
　　I have attempted to hear your will.
　　　　So save me!

3   **You are my last hope.**
4   I offer you myself.
5   **You are forgiving, you are gracious,**
you pour out love for everyone who claims you as a friend.

6   **I really need you, God.**
7   I'm at my wit's end. Doors keep closing on me;
       who else will hear me?
8   You can still rescue me.
       You are God. You alone are God.
9   Eventually, all earthly powers must acknowledge you.
10   **You are great.**

16   **So take pity on me.**
       I'm a child prostitute in the Philippines.
       I'm a forgotten military mistress in Vietnam.
       I'm a starving bag of bones in Somalia,
       I'm a bloodied victim in Sarajevo.
17   Give me a sign.
       Show me that you haven't forgotten me.

PSALM 89:1–4, 19–26
A mother looks at her grown child

*I used exclusively male pronouns in this paraphrase, because I
suspect the feelings may apply more to a grown son than to a
daughter. But please substitute, as you wish.*

1   The miracle never ceases to amaze me, God—
       that this great galumphing galoot came out of me.
       This is my tiny baby—
       this, the next generation of my people.
2   Be with him, God, as you were with me.
3   **You held my hand through the agony of childbirth;**
       through the trials of childrearing, you stayed close beside me.
4   **He's too big for me to carry in my arms any more, God;**
       carry him in yours.

19, 20   Long ago, you anointed David as king,
                when he was just a boy.
         You picked Jeremiah as a prophet,
           before he was even born.
         You claimed Jesus as your own,
           before he was even conceived.

21   **Bless my son too with your special care;**
     hold him in the palm of your hand as he ventures forth.

22   **Do not let him fall into the hands**
         of those who have no conscience.
      Do not let him be mortified by his mistakes.

23   **Clear a path for him through the pitfalls of modern life;**
     let him keep his faith in the decency of all he meets.

24   And God replies: "I will always be with him.
From dewfall to daybreak I will wrap him in a blanket of love;
      from sunrise to sunset, I will help him soar.

25   **I will stay as close to him as the oceans to the shores;**
         I will flow in his veins.

26   **I will be his loving parent;**
         he can always turn to me."

PSALM 89:20–37
Passing on the torch

It's one thing to start a business, an organization, a cause. It's quite another to find the right people to continue it.

20   "I have chosen my successor," says God.
          "I have chosen you.
         You will take my place.

21   For years, I have taught you my vision;
   now I want you to take it forward into the future.

22   **"To avoid being controlled by bureaucrats,**
    to protect yourself against fast-talking promoters
        and bottom-line economists,

23   **you must ask yourself what I would do.**

24   By keeping me always in mind,
    our reputations will both grow.

25   **What I have started, you will continue;**
    through you, my influence will spread.

26   **I have been your launching pad—**

27   Now it's up to you to carry on.

28   **I want to be proud of you.**

29   **As long as you pursue my vision, you will prosper.**

30   "But if you wander off my way,
    if you lust after competitive advantage
    and chase after quick profits,

31   if you sell out to other gods and other goals,

32   **then you will destroy yourself.**
    You will lose all credibility;
    you will go ethically bankrupt.

33   "Even so, I will never turn against you.

34   **I have taken you into my family;**
    you are a member of my household.

35   **I have promised it; I do not lie."**

PSALM 90:1–12, 13–17
A brief pause in the journey

1   Your lantern hangs before our tent.

2   **Its circle of light illuminates this brief stopping place.**
    We do not know where we are going;
    we barely know where we have been.
    We keep our hats handy, always ready to move on.

3   **Perhaps the next campsite will be like this one;**
    perhaps it will not.
    Only you have an overview of our journey.

4   **We are here such a short time.**
    We arrive, we unpack, we explore our environment,
    and then we are gone again.

5   **May the good earth be not harmed by our passage.**
May we be no more dangerous to our planet than a dream
6   that flits across the mind and leaves no mark.
**Like a firefly, bright and brief, we flicker in the darkness,
and then vanish into your warm and holy night.**
9   Like clouds driven before a storm wind, our days scud by;
without a sigh, the last light of the sun winks out in the west.
You drive the wind, you scroll the sun;
you govern the going of our lives.
10   **What does it matter how long we live?
Sometimes it seems too long;**
sometimes it seems as short as a flutter of a butterfly's wings...
12   **It's not how long we live that matters.
But how well.**

13   Do not leave us alone in the dark, Lord.
Take pity on our pathetic emptiness.
14   Light up our days with love,
and let us frolic in the sunshine of your smile.
15   Make our summers as long as our memories;
make winter nights as brief as a whisper.
16   Let us see your inner nature;
lead us into the warm circle of your arms.
17   Shape our attitudes as a potter forms clay.
**Help us become what you envisioned,
when you first thought of us.**

PSALM 91:1–6
Dangerous voyage

There's risk in doing anything. But there's a lot less fear if you have confidence in your car, or boat, or companions.

1   We do not fear uncharted waters.
Our ship is sound, our instruments thoroughly checked.
2   Our skipper knows the sea,
3   and can read the waves like a printed page.

Reefs and shoals reveal their secrets before they can harm us;
4   clear skies assure us of good weather.
5   **What have we to fear?**
6   **Night and day, we are in good hands.**

PSALM 91:9–16
Wishful thinking

*Most of us, I suspect, no longer accept the theology of the
original psalmists that God will protect us from all the hard
knocks of life. But that's what they wrote.*

9   Let your faith be your umbrella;
          Live your life under God's protection.
10   Rain clouds will not ruin your picnics;
      nor will thunderstorms drown your fondest desires.
11   The spirit of God will surround you like a shining shield.
          It will deflect the sticks and stones,
12   and smooth your passage over speed-bumps and potholes.
13   **Neither wind nor sleet nor hail nor snow—**
          nor stress nor illness nor peer pressures—
      shall keep you from growing closer and closer to God.

14   **For God says: "Because you trusted me,**
          I will give you more cause to trust;
          Because you knew me enough to ask for help,
                  I will help you.
15   **When you call, I will answer you.**
          When you fall down, I will pick you up.
16   I will accompany you through a long life;
      I will never leave you lonely and afraid."

PSALM 92:1–4, 12–15
The sacred pines

At Oka, in 1991, the native people considered a grove of pines sacred; the white people did not.

1   As the trees lift their limbs toward heaven,
we raise our faces to the great mystery.
Lone pines become a mighty forest
when we gather to praise you, God.
2   As dew drops cling to the leaves
and sparkle in the morning sun,
our worship reflects bright glimpses of your glory.
3   **We will sing your song like the birds in the branches;**
as persistently as the wind among the pines, we will praise you.
4   **You give us constant cause for joy;**
we see your creation, and happiness dances
like sunshine after a shower.

12   Your people are not shrinking violets;
they stand tall like the sacred pines.
13   Their roots reach deep into the rich soil of your history;
they absorb your being in the air they breathe.
14   Though they have stood for years,
still they hold their heads high.
15   **Their lives reveal God's uprightness.**
God is not a reed, bending to every wind and whim;
God is as reliable as the rocks that form our mountains,
and as satisfying as a running stream in the forests.

PSALM 93
The holy planet

During the Reformation, artist Mathias Grunewald painted what is now called the "Isenheim Altarpiece." Part of it shows God not so much clothed in light as composed of light itself.

1   The Lord wears light like a royal robe;
it dazzles those who gaze upon the Lord.
The whole world is God's royal throne;
like a sapphire, it shines in the darkness of space.
2   The earth has been God's home from the beginning;
before time began, God was there.

3   A river in flood laughs at dykes and sandbags.
Its banks cannot contain it;
it sweeps trees and homes along like dust.
As thundering waters dominate a valley,
4   **so God dominates this planet.**
But God is greater than any flood,
greater than the surf that pounds a rocky shore into sand.
5   For acts of God are not at random;
God rules with justice and fairness,
and makes the whole earth holy.

Hear, oh earth! The Lord, the Lord alone, is God.
Now, and forever.

PSALM 94:12–22
Good students

Some of my strictest school teachers taught me the most.

12   Those whom you discipline are fortunate;
you offer them the opportunity to learn.

    James Taylor

13   Your pupils can crack the endless cycle
of ignorance, of misery, of failure.
They won't need to follow their parents into poverty.

14   Good teachers do not forget their students;
they keep a watchful eye on those they taught.
So does God.
15   God rewards those who make an effort to learn.

16   God asks: "Who's paying attention to me?
Who will follow my instructions?"
17   **I am tempted to stay silent.**
I do not want to be called on.
But God's eye is upon me; I cannot look away.
18   My knees knock with fear.
I would fall down, but God holds me up.
19   I am burdened by my own inadequacies;
they weigh me down; they keep me off balance.
But God gives me confidence.

20   It's hard to admit what we don't know, God.
Good pupils learn from their mistakes;
poor pupils refuse to admit they have made mistakes.
People in power always claim to have the answers,
but their answers always serve their own interests.
21   They conspire together to preserve their own privileges.
They prey on those who have no power, no voice, no place.
In the name of stability,
they condemn the helpless to continued suffering.

22   **Lord, you are my teacher.**
Teach me to know right from wrong,
to know the easy answers from the truth.
Even when it hurts.

PSALM 95:1–7
The devotion of a special pet

Once, we had a little dog who always greeted our arrival with overflowing joy, even if we had been away for only a few minutes.

1   We run to our maker like ecstatic puppies.
God is our hope, our strength.
2   **We come before God with our whole beings quivering.**
We have no words worth using;
we whimper with happiness.
3   **For our God is great and good.**
There is no one greater.
4   **When God speaks, we would not dream of disobeying.**
5   When God steps into the street, cars come to a standstill;
flowers look up in their beds;
weeds wilt in their lawns.
6   **So we pour ourselves out on the ground before God;**
we lie down and wriggle with delight;
we jump into the air with joy.
7   **For this great God is *our* God.**
We belong to God;
we are beloved members of God's household.
When God whistles, we come running.

PSALM 95:8–11
The risks of disobedience

Regardless of good intentions, pets are not always obedient!

8   God issues a warning: "Do not test my patience.
9   **Your parents knew my authority,**
but still they tried to get their own way.
10   They obeyed me to my face," God says,
"But behind my back, they broke my rules.
11   **So I banished them from my house.**
From now on, they sleep in the doghouse."

PSALM 95
Unity with creation

1   Come and climb up to the top of the rock;
stand on top, and stretch your arms out to the sky.
2   Reach out to the holiness
that wraps its breath around you.
In grateful silence, soak up the shining light of life.
3   God is the rock upon which we live;
4   **all the earth is God's.**
From ocean abyss to mountain pinnacle,
5   **from polar icefield to tropical rain forest,**
God lives in every subtle link of life.
6   **Bow your head before the wonder of it all;**
feel the strength of the rock rise through your feet.
7   **We are not alone;**
we are one in God.
**Lichens and trees, ants and people—
all are held in the palm of God's hand.**

8   Do not isolate yourself from God's creation.
Do not consider your concerns first.
9   You will cut yourself off from God who created you;
you will think of yourself as god.
10   Your struggles will lead you farther astray;
you will sink farther into a morass of your own making.
11 In your loneliness, you will begin to believe that there is no God;
you will never know the peace that passes understanding.

PSALM 96
A hero's welcome

*For a taste of the welcome Israel had in mind for the promised
Messiah, imagine a team coming home with Olympic gold
medals or a world championship.*

1   Prepare the streets for the parade!
          Put up more bunting; hang up more flags!
2   The one we honor is coming home;
              our hero is returning.
3   We want everyone to know how we feel;
    we want our neighbors to share our celebration.
4   For our hero is unique.
5   **Others put their faith in individuals,**
              in weapons or armies,
         in economic or political systems.
   We put our faith in the creator of heaven and earth.

6   Mere human praise pales before the creator of all life.
7   **Words are not enough—**
      we must put our feelings into actions.
8   We wave flags; we hang bunting;
             we crowd along the curbs.
9   **Our actions will change nothing—**
        the outcome is already decided—
10   **but they help to express our feelings.**

11   The whole world should be cheering with us:
   let the earth wave palm branches in praise;
          let the air fill with rainbows;
12   **let spirits burn as bright as fire;**
    and water wash clean the sands of time.
13   **For our creator is coming back to us**
        to take control of creation.

PSALM 96
The light shines

The lectionaries suggest this as a reading at Christmas.

1 Softly, as in a winter sunrise,
a line of light breaks the blackness of the night.
2 **The song the Singer sang at creation—**
the high sweet melody heard only inside the soul—
shimmers in the frosty air.
3 At last the long night is over.
The glory of the new day spills into the expectant skies.

4 God rewards the vigil of the sleepless watchers.
5 **But those who dissipated their energies**
in "midnight madness" sales
now see that their goods are defective.
Their gaudy packages are all empty.
6 **True worth never comes from consuming;**
it comes only from God.

7 **Fall on your knees, with your face to the rising sun;**
give thanks for new beginnings.
8 **Fall on your knees, with your face to the rising Son,**
and offer yourself as a gift to the child.
9 **For the light shines in the darkness,**
and the darkness can never overcome it.

10 Wake up, and welcome the new day!
11 **The birds sing, the buds blossom,**
even glaciers melt their frozen hearts;
12 **trees lift bare arms to the light.**
13 For God has come to live among us.
God will demonstrate the way of righteousness;
the living God will reveal truth for all time.

PSALM 97
Power beyond comprehension

1   From coast to coast, from earth to sky,
God is in charge.

2   **God judges the earth with justice and fairness.**

      Look up and see the pillars of God's palace,
the black clouds boiling above the burning peaks.

3   **God's hammer strikes their brooding anvils,
and lightning leaps across the skies;**

4   judgment thunders, and the earth trembles.

5   **Even the mountains melt.**
Glowing lava rolls down like a mighty river;

6   volcanoes spray the skies with fire.

God is surrounded by flame, far above our comprehension.

7   Who else could create such a spectacle?

Who would choose to worship anything less?

8   God's people rejoice;

God's people are confident their faith is justified.

9   You, God, tower above earthly things;

you tower over our cultural idols, our golden calves.

10   And yet you, God, reach out with gentle hands
to those who struggle against sinful ways.

11   **For those who walk in your way,
a ray of light beams through the densest clouds.**

12   So rejoice in the Lord, and give thanks.

PSALM 97
Order in chaos

1 There is more here than mere chaos.
We cannot understand this misery—
but it would be worse if there was no cause, no purpose.
It cannot be just random chance.
2 The shells rain down upon our cities;
clouds of destruction boil into the sky.
3 The onslaught darkens the day with smoke;
it makes the night flicker with fire.
4 The rocket's red glare slashes open the tomb of darkness;
the ground beneath us trembles to the impact of the mortars.
5 Buildings collapse, as if the earth
had been pulled out from beneath them;
windows shatter into vicious lances;
no place is safe any more.

6 **In the midst of this devastation,**
we still believe in a God of justice and fairness;
we believe in the God who brought order out of chaos.
7 **We need to believe that somehow, someone is in control.**
The God we worship is not a graven image
carved out of our own egos.
8 **If we are right, our children have a future;**
we can rejoice for them.
9 If God were our creation, we would have no hope but in ourselves;
we would have no hope at all.
But we are God's creation.
We can trust that God is greater than our present pain.

10 God has plans for those who cause others to suffer,
for those who advance their own cause through violence.
But the innocent will inherit a peace that passes understanding.
11 In that confidence, we can go out into our shattered streets.
We can share what little we have with each other.
12 We are most favored of the Lord,
for we have learned what God is like.

PSALM 98
The Lord will come

*When King David brought the Ark of the Covenant to Jerusalem,
he danced and sang in celebration. It was a grand and glorious
procession—a parade, in our terms.*

1   It's time to show our appreciation
         to the one who saved us from humiliation.
2   **Our foes thought they could wipe their feet on us,**
         but God didn't let us become doormats.
3   It's time to show our feelings;
         it's time to make a joyful noise!

         Is everyone ready?
5   Then strike up the band!
6   **Trumpets and clarinets carry the tune;**
         Drums pound the beat; piccolos pierce the air;
         trombones and tubas growl their counterpoint.

         The earth itself will join this jam session!
7   Ocean surf adds the rhythm of its roar,
8   **winds wail a descant around mountain spires,**
         and raging rivers rumble rocks deep in their valleys.
         Let the whole of creation rise to a crescendo—
9   **and then fall silent.**
         For the Lord comes.

The Lord comes to judge the world, and all who live in it.
The Lord judges with fairness and compassion.
The Lord loves.
But the Lord also judges.

         James Taylor

PSALM 98
Togetherness

*Some families are happy, some are tragic. Yet we all have a
vision of what family life could be like. On Christmas morning,
our family opened our stockings together in the bedroom.*

1   Grandparents perch on the edge of the bed;
young children snuggle in beside their parents.

2   **The family circle is unbroken;
everyone belongs here.**
It is a time of expectation and of celebration.

3   **Wherever they go, whatever they do,
members of this family will be faithful to each other.**
They will always be each other's children,
always each other's parents.

4   **They all talk at once, excitedly;**
when they hear themselves, they burst into laughter.

5   **Laughter is the icing on a cake of comfort
that many generations have baked;**
it tinkles around the room like glass bells hung on a tree.

6   **As cold toes grow warmer under a comfy quilt,
so loving relationships grow warmer with time.**

7   Though icy winds howl and blizzards rage,
children will wriggle and seniors smile gently.

8   **The simple pleasures of companionship
rise from them to heaven;**
it is a sacrifice pleasing to God,

9   **for God loves a loving relationship,
and judges the quality of our lives together.**

PSALM 98
The great dance of creation

1   How different God's creation is from human conflict.
The clamor of human strife creates a cacophony.

Like orchestras competing with their conductor,
nations murder each other's melodies.
2   **But God has other music.**
3   The colors of nature never clash with each other.
4   **In a garden, every shade of leaf and flower
joins in a joyous chorus;**
bare branch and bonsai provide a counterpoint
balancing the beauty of blossoms.
5, 6   **In the depths of the jungle,
the sounds of termite and tiger weave a wondrous harmony;**
eerie descants echo through the ocean's deeps;
the rhythm of life throbs in every cell,
and the seasons swell and ebb away.
7, 8   **From the farthest nebula to the tiniest atom,
all creation dances to honor its choreographer.**
9   And God applauds each performance.

PSALM 99
At the foot of the mountains

*Ancient peoples looked up to the fearful heights of mountain
peaks as the habitation of the gods.*

1   Like a halo of holiness, the spirit of God envelops the earth.
In the deep stillness of space, God's spirit gives life;
let us acknowledge our insignificance.
In the emptiness of infinity, God's spirit creates life;
let us acknowledge our interdependence.

2   Look up if you would see God;
raise your sights beyond repetitive routines.
3   But do not attempt to face God as an equal—
**fling yourself face down on the earth
before the creator of the heavens.**

4   Almighty God, you love to do right.
In your dealings with your creation, you are always fair.

5   **We humans grovel before your greatness.**
Humbly, we kiss the earth from which you fashioned us.
You are holiness itself.

6   The humus holds the recycled cells
of those who came this way before us.
Step by step they searched for you, until you found them.

7   By pillar of fire and by whispering breeze,
by bonfire and whirlwind, by prophecy and parable,
you showed them your way.

8   **Because they tried to follow you,
you forgave them their failings.**

9   **So come—pledge allegiance to our God!**
Gather at the foot of the mountain,
where even the rocks reach up towards our God.
God, you are holiness itself.

PSALM 99
Out of the ruts

For this paraphrase, I borrowed some ideas from Paul's Letter to the Philippians (4:8).

1   Raise your sights from the ruts of routine;
look up, look up, to the Lord who stands above everything.

2   For God is greater than any abstract theory,
any set of principles or moral values.

3   **God embodies all that is right and good.**

4   Whatever is true, honest, and just,
whatever is pure, lovely, and admirable—
if it deserves praise or commendation, it is of God.

5   **But we mortals keep our heads down.**
Like ants at a picnic, we busy ourselves with crumbs
and miss the bigger picture.
God is too great for us to grasp.

6 We know God through the lives of those who have known God.
7   **Our spiritual ancestors**
   stumbled over God's unexpected presence;
   When they stubbed their toes, God forgave them
8   because they were willing to learn.
   God watched over them, guiding their feet.

9   In God, we find the ultimate example
   of how we should act towards others.

PSALM 100
God's playground

Children, unself-consciously exuberant, best convey the sheer joy of this psalm.

1   Leap and dance with joy—
   . **the showers have ended, the sun has come out again.**
2   Splash through the puddles!
   Roll in the grass!
   Let laughter rise in the air like flights of sparrows!
3   This is God's world!
   God made it, God made us—and it is good!
   We spoil it if we stare at it through sour faces.
   God set us free to frolic, to gambol,
   to celebrate the gift of life.
4   So dance your way down the garden;
   scatter rose-petals with every step.
   With every breath, enjoy the goodness of God!
5   **From the beginning of time, God has poured out love;**
   God will continue loving 'til time stops ticking.

PSALM 100
The dance of life

Even when I forget the steps and foul up the patterns, square dancing is fun.

1   Two guitars and a washtub bass,
            a country fiddle, an old-time caller.
        Come on, everyone, join the dance.
2   Do-si-do and allemande left,
        swing your partner, bow to your corner.
        Clap those hands and stamp those feet.

3   God calls the square dance of our lives;
    God swirls our varied colors like a kaleidoscope.
    We dance our complex patterns to God's grand design.
4   **Step onto God's dance floor with a song in your heart
            and a smile on your face,**
5   for God loves a good time too.
        God is in the sweat and the swinging,
        in the sawdust and the singing.
            God *is* the dance of life.
    Whether you join the dance or sit on the sidelines,
                the beat goes on,
        and fills the night with music!

PSALM 101
Good intentions

Like teenagers who promise to clean up their rooms and their habits, we rarely manage to keep all our promises. But aren't good intentions better than nothing?

1   God, I want to be worthy of you.
2   **I want to do whatever it takes to win your love.**
        I will clean up my heart, my mind, my spirit;
        I will shine and polish my soul for you.

3a **I will not hunger for personal power;**
I will not lust for winning lottery tickets;
4 I will not be swayed by public opinion polls or peer pressures;
I will banish selfish motives from my life.
3b **I will not associate with those**
who seek only their own satisfaction;
I reject their attitudes;
I do not want them to rub off on me.
5 When gossip flies, I will close my ears;
I will not tolerate pride or prejudice in anyone.
6 **I will choose for my friends**
those who have a strong faith, and who live by it;
we shall support each other as we walk forward together.
7 I will have nothing to do with pretense;
transparent honesty must mark all my relationships.
I will not tolerate lies—even little white lies.
8 In this way, day by day,
I will detach myself from those who deny God.
1 **God, I want to be worthy of you.**
2 **I want to do whatever it takes to win your love.**

PSALM 102:1–11
Life reduced to ashes

Some days, we really get the blues!

1 Lord, you've got to listen!
It's because of you that I'm calling!
2 Don't look the other way;
you know who I am;
you know why I'm here.
I need some answers. Now!

3 Throw some dry grass on a fire—that's how I feel:
a puff of smoke dispersed on the breeze,
a flash of heat that fades as fast as it came.
4 There's nothing left in my life but ashes.

I sift through them, looking for the person I used to be.
6   **I'm blown about by every wind,**
drifting across sterile parking lots,
piling up against curbs.
5   The thunder rolls; the rains sluice down;
my ashes turn into grey glue.

7   **I'm doomed to drift all through my days.**
8   No one wants me; no one cares about me;
no one even speaks kindly of me.
9   I worry all day.
Everything I eat tastes like ashes;
everything I drink sets my teeth on edge.

10   And it's all because of you.
You and I were close once.
Then you dumped me;
you turned your back on me.
11   **Now I have a black cloud hanging over me.**
All my life is lived in shadow.

PSALM 102:2–12
Lament of a cast-off lover

2   Listen to me, God!
You are harder to reach than a politician
hiding behind a smokescreen of words;
you are as secluded as a CEO
protected by secretaries and receptionists.
3   I cannot afford to waste any more time waiting.
My time is limited;
life is leaving me, like a puff of smoke in the wind.
4   **I've lost my appetite.**
My heart is empty.
5   My joints creak.
6   **My life has become a wasteland,**
a compost bin for high hopes.

7   I can't sleep.

8   **I prowl the halls at night,**
without even a shadow to keep me company.

9   Bread tastes like ashes;
the finest wine turns to vinegar in my mouth.

10   And it's all your fault.
You left me.
You dumped me like yesterday's coffee grounds.

11   Because of you, I have become a shadow of my former self.

12   **They tell me you're doing fine.**
I wish I could see you sometime.

PSALM 103:1–18
A breath of hope

1   My heart races; blood rushes to my face.

·2   ·´ · **I feel myself glowing for the goodness of God.**

3   For God accepts me in spite of my shortcomings;
God strengthens me to rise above my failures.

4   God plucks me out of the pit of despair and self-pity,
and lets me enjoy the spring sun.

5   **God finds me friends to stimulate my mind;**
how can I vegetate when they keep me alive?

6   If you're weary, heavy-laden, God will give you rest;
if you're under someone's thumb, God will set you free.

7   Don't be doubtful—look at God's history;
Time after time, God has rescued us from crisis.

8   God's love is gentle and kind;
it rarely resorts to anger;
like a mighty river, it runs deep and dependable.

9   God does not hold grudges.

10   **God does not simply treat us as we deserve,**
for our faults deserve correction,
and our continued failings deserve punishment.

11   **But those are human judgments;**
God is as different from us as air is from water.
12   **God buries our shortcomings;**
they might as well be at the bottom of the sea.
13   **As a parent takes pity on an erring child,**
as a youngster welcomes home a wandering puppy,
so God's arms are always open to us.

PSALM 103:19–22
Hold high the good name

"Bless the Lord," says the traditional wording of this psalm. But how can humans bless God? I settled on a secondary meaning of "bless"—to make sacred, to sanctify, to hallow.

20   **Hold high the good name of God!**
Hallow it, you who shake free of earthly shackles,
you birds and butterflies,
you spirits of saints past and saints possible.
Your response is not bound by human limitations.

21   **Hold high the good name of God!**
Hallow it, all who walk upon the earth.
Witness to God's will in your daily work.

22   **Hold high the good name of God;**
Hallow it, the whole of God's creation,
all who creep and crawl,
all who reach blindly from the soil towards the light.
Hold high the good name of God;

hallow it, my life.

PSALM 104:1–9
Fertile imagination

1   Actors strut at the front of the stage
before their sets and props.
Behind the whole production stands the director.
2   You, God, are the director of our dramas.
Within your mind, we exist;
we laugh, we cry, we play, we work.
Without you, we would be nothing.

3, 4   For you said, "Let there be..."
And there was.
The skies, the seas, the clouds, the hills—
all sprout from your fertile imagination.

5   When the universe began its vast explosion,
you were there.
6   When the spinning galaxies scattered through space,
you were there.
7   When the solar system strung its diamond necklace in the sky
you were there.
8   When life emerged on one frail planet,
you were there.
9   When the spirit of holiness lived among us,
you were there.

Without you, we would be nothing.

       James Taylor

PSALM 104:14–18
Consolation

I suspect that, deep down, our greatest fear is that we could vanish without being noticed.

14, 15   **We are no more than dandelion fluff.**
One minute we stand proud in the sun—
we think we have it all together.

16   **The next, the wind plucks us from our perch**
and scatters us, wherever.

17   Yet God has purposes, even for fluff.
Not one of us perishes pointlessly.

18   God does not forget us, or ignore us.
To God's faithful, God is always faithful.

PSALM 104:24–34
Our place in creation

24   You made everything, God.
You imagine it, and it happens.
You breathe on it and give it life.

25   **The oceans are the amniotic fluid of the earth.**
In your womb we share our origins.

26   **We like to think we look after ourselves**
with trade and commerce,
with boats that plow the seas,
with trains and trucks and planes.
We braid our lives with busy-ness.

27   **Yet everything owes its life to you;**
everything continues to depend on you for life.

28   **You bring forth food from the earth,**
from the seas, from the skies.
By your bounty all are fed.

29   **If you withdraw your favor,**
we all perish.

Without you, we are no more
than a collection of chemicals.
30 **But you put your breath of life into us.**
With each new generation, you renew us.
31 **Our living bodies reveal your spirit.**
May our living be acceptable to you, our Lord.

32 **You create the volcanoes and the earthquakes,**
the hurricanes and glaciers;
you shape the earth itself.
33 **Yet you care about us.**
We are overwhelmed with gratitude.

34 **This is our understanding—**
may it meet with your approval.

PSALM 105:1–11
Stewardship of life

*Flying across the country overnight, you can sometimes see the
light of dawn spreading across the darkened lands below.*

1b The still earth stirs to the touch of God;
fresh light spills across the resting lands.
2 Waken the sleepers to share in the wonder;
sing praises to the creator, all you people.
1a Give thanks, give thanks to God.
3 **The glory of dawn rises over the horizon;**
our hearts rise in response.
4 **Look, see how the wonders extend to the edge of the world;**
everywhere, the glory of God bursts into being.
5 **Each new day is a miracle.**

God watches over the world, from the east to the west,
and banishes fears of darkness.
6 **Yet this same God chooses to watch over us;**

7   this is the wonder of the Lord our God—
the creator of the universe,
the ruler of earth, the life of all lands—
8   **this God cares about us,**
and about our children, and our children's children.
9   **This God also cared about our ancestors,**
about our ancestors' ancestors,
long before we existed.
10   God made promises to us. God will keep those promises.
11   **God said, "I will give you this land.**
Pass it on to your children, and to your children's children.
Take care of it."

PSALM 105:1–6
Borrowed glory: 1

Our team won the World Series; our candidate wins the election;
our scientist wins a Nobel Prize... and we act as if we had
something to do with it.

    These verses are the opening for a series of readings from
this psalm, all expressing gratitude for being part of a noble
lineage. The paraphrases attempt to catch the feeling of the
original in contemporary contexts.

1   Here they come!
We rise to our feet—
we give them a standing ovation.
In the coffee shop, in the shopping mall, in the churches,
we discuss their wonderful deeds.
2   We organize a parade down Main Street in their honor;
we proclaim their greatness in every newspaper and broadcast.
3   They make us proud of ourselves.
4   **We press close around them;**
we collect their autographs.
5   **For they have performed miracles;**
they have done more than we dreamed they could.

6 **We share in their fame—**
we bask in their glory,
for we come from the same roots.
16 **We have waited a long time for this recognition;**
we shall revel in every delicious moment of it.

PSALM 105:17–22
Borrowed glory: 2

*Roberta Bondar spent years in obscurity, training to be an
astronaut. After her mission, she became an instant celebrity.*

17 We have had our hopes raised before.
We invested our faith in saviors.
We put them on pedestals, but they let us down;
they had clay feet.
We turned on them;
18 like jackals, we tore their reputations apart.
19 But one of them became famous, after all.
20 **We praised her to the heavens;**
at luncheons and dinners,
we sat her in the place of honor.
21 **We elected her to high office;**
she endorsed luxury cars on television.
22 **She was invited to talk to students in school assemblies;**
in our eyes, she could do nothing wrong.
45 She brought us great honor.

PSALM 105:23–26, 45C
Borrowed glory: 3

*Canadian authors have to win acclaim internationally before we
are willing to honor them locally.*

23 We are Margaret Atwood's extended family;
we are Robertson Davies' friends.

Once we had doubts about them;
we turned a cold shoulder to their abilities.
24 **But God must have favored them.**
God made them famous.
25 **God had plans for them;**
surely God included us in those plans.
Of course they alienated a few crackpots along the way,
26 **but we are not among them, thank God.**
We belong to the charmed circle;
we are their friends, their family.
We will make them national idols.

PSALM 105:37–45
Borrowed glory: 4

37 We had a strong leader.
We thought we were rich then,
with pots of money for social programs
with oil and gas to burn.
38 We threw him out of office
39 for he set our teeth on edge—
we hated the sight of him.
His policies cast a cloud across our land.
40 **He gave us a constitution and a charter;**
he freed us from our colonial past.
41 The money gushed out.

42 Now we remember him.
We read his memoirs and watch him on television.
43 We wonder what happened to strong leaders.
44 **We look for heroes among our has-beens,**
and long for another Moses
to lead us to our promised land.

PSALM 106:1–5, 7–15, 19–22, 23
Character sketches

To balance Psalm 105, which boasts about history, Psalm 106 reviews the same story as confession. I read it as collection of not always flattering character sketches.

A fawning lackey grovels for favor

1   Congratulations, Lord.
          You achieved your goals magnificently.
2   But who am I to brag about your achievements?
      I'm only a small cog in your mighty machinery.
4   **Still, don't forget me.**
       I played a small part in your success.
5   **If it's all right with you,**
      I'd like to share in some of your glory.
3   You should reward those who didn't rock your boat,
      who didn't break down under pressure,
        who didn't foul up the process.
4 **When you hand out rewards, please remember me.**

A doubter remains unconvinced

5   I'd like to believe you.
8   But I must be objective.
      We had a pretty good life back there—
        why do we need to change?
9–12   So you parted the sea and you walked on the waters;
      you conquered our foes and you pardoned the sinners.
       You gave us a land and you led us to comfort;
    you gave us self-confidence—we thought you were great!

13   **But so what?**
     We're headed for hell in a handcart again.
14   Everything's falling apart;
     everyone's greedy, and no one trusts anyone.
15   **We're no better off than we were.**

6   We have made bad decisions;
         we have pursued harmful policies.

7   We sold our country and our culture
         to curry favor with our competitors;
         we traded our birthright for a mess of promises.
         It seemed expedient at the time.

19   Our companies making weapons
         profited from the misery of helpless people.

20   **We wrote God into our constitution**
         and wrote God out of our culture.

21   **We have no room for God in economics and politics.**

22   We have forgotten what God has done in the past;
         we have assumed that God will not act in the future.

We all ask for absolution

23   Now God is angry.
         Please God, do not destroy us.
         Remember that you called us your children;
         remember that you said you love us.

PSALM 107:1–9
The testimony of the refugees

There are almost 30 million refugees—wandering in the wilderness.

1   Speak up, you who believe in the Lord;
         give thanks to God, for God is good;
         God never stops loving.

2   Say it publicly.
         If we fail to tell of God's goodness,
         how will anyone know?

3   We are the people of God, wherever we are:
         north or south, east or west, rich or poor, powerful or helpless.

4   We wander homeless among people who don't want us,

we drift like ice floes in the Arctic.

5   We lack food and drink;

we lack companionship and compassion;

we are ready to give up.

6   **But you heard our cries, Lord.**

You gave us a sense of our own worth.

7   **You pointed us towards a new home;**

we will dwell in the house of our Lord forever.

8   **This is our story, and this is our God.**

9   God sustains us.

When we are thirsty, we receive something to drink;

when we are hungry, we are fed.

Thanks be to God.

PSALM 107:1–3, 17–22
Those who know

Feel free to substitute names and places currently in the news.

2, 3   All around the world, millions will attest—

1   God will not let you down.

17   **Sometimes that seems hard to believe.**

Hatred robs black South Africans of hope.

The bias of international mass media

makes Palestinians feel despised and rejected;

they hide their faces from us.

Weapons of war maim women and children in Rwanda.

Poverty pursues refugees from Sri Lanka,

and starvation the Kurds from Iraq.

18   **Fear and despair crushes them.**

19   **But God gives them strength to continue.**

20   God heals the raw wounds in their souls;

God holds them gently in their nightmares.

21   They do not doubt God's saving grace.

22   **Listen to them! Hear their story!**

Hear, and believe, and rejoice.

          James Taylor

PSALM 107:23–37
Tragedy into triumph

23   There are those who go downtown,
        risking their fortunes daily on the stock market.

24   **They believed no harm could come to them;**
        they believed the myth of constant growth.

25   **But the markets rode a roller-coaster.**

26   The stocks rose to new records,
        and the stocks came crashing down.
        In the blink of an eyelid,
        in the blip of a computer screen,
        they saw their fortunes vanish.

27   They clutched their throats, they held their hearts.

28   **They cried out to their bankers for help,**
        and the banks foreclosed on their mortgages.

        They cried out to God for help,
        and God calmed their stormy spirits.

29   **They found peace within themselves.**
        They took time for their families and friends.

30   Then they saw that their tragedy was not all bad.

31   **They were grateful for a second chance**

32   **to get their priorities straightened out.**

33   God could have made them squirm.
        God could have given them parapets to jump off,
        and traffic to rush into.

34   That might have served them right.

35   **But God prefers to turn stagnant waters**
        into sparkling streams,
        and tragedies into triumphs.

36   **For a new life is better than none,**

37   and a renewed life witnesses to God's wisdom.

PSALM 107:33–38, 43
In an ideal world

33   God could easily turn a summer day into a blizzard,
        a wedding celebration into a funeral,
34   a placid pond into quicksand,
        a family reunion into a civil war.
        But God does not do such things;
        God's love never wavers.
35   God turns sandboxes into gardens,
        and slums into communities of joy.
36 **In God's intended world, foxes have holes, birds have nests,**
        and refugees have roofs over their heads.
37   Fields are free to forage in,
        and trees bend over with fruit.
        Ocean shoals abound with cod and scallops.
38   **In God's intended world,**
        all creatures live in harmony with each other.

43   Let those who have ears to hear, hear.
        Let them remember that God's love never wavers.

PSALM 110
A higher viewpoint

For hikers, there's a special thrill in making it to the top of a pass or a peak, and seeing over the other side.

1   Come, says God.
        Come and sit beside me.
2   **From up here, you seem to see forever.**
        The world unfurls like a lush carpet,
        a banquet of beauty spread before you.
3   **If people everywhere could share this viewpoint,**
        they might not focus on their own feet
        plodding along their dusty paths.
        Cares and causes choke them.

**If they could cast their narrow concerns aside,
they could drink air fresh as morning dew in the mountains.**
Like a baby bursting from its mother's womb,
they could gulp the first breaths of a new life.

4   **God makes that promise.**
And God does not break promises.
5   **If God can grind the mighty mountains down,
and spread their silt across the plains,**
6   then surely God can also topple temporary governments,
and grind dictatorships into dust,
and turn off the toxins of industrial wantonness.

7   **Come, says God.**
Come and sit beside me.
Drink deeply of the pure waters of my creation.
Lift your eyes from the dust, and look, and see.

PSALM 111
The weaver

*As with some other psalms, I felt impelled here to use a personal
pronoun, but this time it was "she" rather than "he."*

1   Where should I praise God?
Among God's people, of course!
2   For God does great things.
3   **God's handiwork is beautiful; it will not rot or fade.**
Those who can see God's artistry will study it.
4   **They will recognize God's reality in their lives.**
And God will remember them, for God is gracious and kind.

5   God looks after her friends; she keeps her promises.
6   **She does not flaunt her skill
but demonstrates it in countless daily ways;**
she constantly shares her power with her people.
7   **God weaves our threads together on the loom of life;**

like a seamless garment are God's standards.
8   **The works of God's hands will last;**
       whatever God does is done well.

9   **God teaches her people well;**
           she has made a commitment to us.
           God keeps her promises,
           and expects us to keep our promises too.
10   **A healthy respect for God is the beginning of wisdom;**
       wisdom will lead to a better relationship with God.
           Let us praise God every day.

PSALM 111
An awesome responsibility

1   The bright blue planet spins in the vast darkness of space;
       let all who live on the earth rejoice.
2   Only on this one small ball do we know life exists;
       let all who live on the earth give thanks.
3   The vision takes our breath away;
       let all who live on the earth open their eyes.
4   This fragile ball bursting with life is a work of art;
       let all who live on earth recognize God's goodness.
5   Foxes and fieldmice, humans and whales, eagles and ants—
       all are woven together in a tapestry of relationships;
       let all who live on the earth recognize this reality.
6   And God has delegated responsibility to us;
       let all who live on the earth be mindful.
7   All life is balanced in a delicate equilibrium;
    let all who live on the earth understand their responsibility.
8   A tapestry cannot be reduced to a single thread;
    let all who live on the earth accept their responsibility.
9   This egg floating in the dark womb of the universe
           is like God's own embryo;
       let all who live on the earth treat it as holy.
10   We share an awesome and terrible responsibility;
       may God live forever.

PSALM 112:1–9
Fair exchange

1   Those who trust God's wisdom,
and who are willing to learn God's ways,
will never be ground down by their problems.
2   **They will refer to their children with pride;**
they will receive respect from all.
3   Their influence will extend far beyond their own circles.
4   **In trials and tribulations, God will give them help—**
but not before they require it,
or they might rely on themselves instead of God.

5   **In return, God expects them**
to share their skills and talents generously,
to treat everyone fairly,
to lighten the loads of sufferers.
6   Because they know who and what they are,
their heads are not turned by every trend and fad.
7   **They are not broken by bad news.**
8   Misfortune does not destroy them,
for they weigh their worth by other scales.
9   **Whatever they have, they use for the common good;**
when they die, they are remembered with gratitude.

PSALM 113:1–9
Thank-you letters

Do you remember, as a child, writing letters to relatives for their Christmas and birthday gifts?

1   Dear God,
How can we thank you enough for your gifts to us?
2   **We will remember you with gratitude**
today, and tomorrow, and all through the days to come.
3   All day, every day, we will thank you.
4   **You saw our situation. You noticed our needs.**

7   You brightened our lives with your gifts.
You lifted us up to sit in your lap.
You made us feel loved and wanted.
5   **You looked on us with love.**
6   **There is no one else like you;**
you understand the deepest yearnings of our hearts.
8   **We are wealthy beyond our wildest imaginings.**
9   Last night our home was bitter and sad;
today it rings with laughter and joy
because you chose us as your family.

PSALM 114:1–8
Because of you

1   This morning, the skies were grey;
the north wind blew bleak and cold.
2   Then I met you.
3   And the sun came out;
the roses burst into bloom;
the birds began singing;
4   **the storm clouds retreated across the horizon.**
5   Because of you.

6   **You changed my life;**
just by being here, you transformed my world.
7 **Before you came, I could not see the sun, nor hear the birds.**
Now the feet that dragged their way through dreary days
have learned to dance.
Stumbling blocks have turned into cornerstones.
8   The ice that held my heart in a wintry grip has melted
and joy pours out of me like a fountain.
Because of you.

    James Taylor

PSALM 115:1–18
The limitations of laws

Of course we need laws. But we also need love.

1   Don't you care about your reputation, Lord?
           They're calling you a wimp, a gutless wonder.
             They question your existence.
2   "Show us your God," the scornful insist;
              "Prove it!" the skeptics demand.
        They won't be satisfied with ancient stories.

3   Our God is invisible, we explain.
          Our God is out there and in here,
            in heaven and in hearts.
How can we show him to you when you refuse to see him?

4   **But you do not look for a personality;**
    you expect rules and regulations, laws and legislation.
5   **Rigid rules and inflexible regulations speak—**
            but they can never listen;
      they can command, but they cannot care.
6   **They judge, but never understand;**
       they demand, but can't sympathize.
7   **Laws never shed tears of joy when a baby is born,**
    never smell the dewy earth on an autumn morning,
    never burst into spontaneous song on a forest path.
8   **Laws are as fallible as the people who make them.**
9   Universal truth comes only from the creator of the universe,
        the God of galaxies and mustard seeds,
          of supernovas and fruit flies.

10   If you profess to be the people of God,
11   don't depend on laws, or science, or technology,
            to solve your problems—
              depend on God.

12   God has been good to us;
    even through the bad times, we had nothing to fear;
          we knew God was right there with us.
13 Our elders and our children found strength when they needed it.
14   **God's love is not doled out like soup;**
                it is not a pie to be portioned.
    The more each person has, the more there is for everyone.
15   **God made the past, the present, and the future;**
              God makes all three meaningful.
16   **We need not wait impatiently for the future—**
              God has given us the present.
17   We need not wait until we die to know paradise;
              God offers the best of life right here.
18 **Once you taste the zest of life with God, even for a moment,**
              you will never doubt again.

PSALM 116:1–9
Recovery from rock bottom

Alcoholics Anonymous teaches that you can only change when you hit bottom.

1   When I was lost, God found me.
        When I was alone, God walked with me.
2   When I was desperately lonely, God listened to me
              while I poured out my soul.
          God is my lifelong friend now.
3   I was ready to give up;
        I had nothing to live for any more;
          I was so bone-weary I could have died.
4   **When I hit bottom, I turned my life over to God.**
5   And God was kind; God accepted my offer.
6   **I could not have done it when I was full of confidence;**
              I could not have let go.
    But when I sensed the earth itself disintegrating under me,
              I had no more pride—
                I cried out for help.

7   **And God took my hand and held me up.**

8   God saved me from the grave.

God wiped away my tears, and taught me to walk again.

9   I'm back in the land of the living,

but I will continue to walk with God.

PSALM 116:1–4, 12–19
Gratitude

1   God knows how to listen.

2   **Others hear only their own voices;**

they recognize only the empty echoes of their own desires.

But God heard me when I cried out.

I will never forget that.

3   I had given up hope.

4   **As a last resort, I called to God.**

"Save me," I cried. "Rescue me from this mess!"

12   How can I thank God?

13   **Since I owe God every breath of my new life,**

I dedicate every breath to God—

every glass of water, every bite of bread.

14   I will not be silenced.

I shall pry open the shells of privacy

that people build around themselves;

In crowded elevators or on windblown corners

I will whisper my message

into ears stoppered with self-interest.

15   **I will say, "God loves each and every one of us.**

Every person who believes in God is precious."

16, 17   **I have nothing to lose.**

All that I am, I owe to God.

18   I don't care what my convictions cost me;

19 **From the edges of civilization to the center of the universe,**

I will glorify this God who saves.

PSALM 116:1–2, 12–19
God as grandmother

*The little girl's eyes suddenly lit up. "Nana!" she said, pointing,
"Nana!" And she ran to her grandmother, who had just come in.*

1   Granny listens to me.
       I tell her my stories, and she believes me.
2   When others blame me, Granny doesn't jump to conclusions.
         She doesn't get upset;
         she doesn't always support someone else.
         She really listens to me.
12   How do I thank her?
13   **By running to her with my arms stretched out**
         whenever I see her.

15   Granny says I'm precious.
16   **Everyone else expects me to do things their way.**
         But she doesn't expect me to be anyone but myself.
         I would do anything to make her happy.
17   I help her set the table, without being asked.
         I help her crack eggs for the pan;
         I like making beds with her.
18   **Even when she has company visiting,**
         I fling my arms around her neck and hug her.
19   I love going to Granny's house.

         I hope God is like my Granny.

PSALM 117
Mantra

*This psalm is so short, it made me think of a mantra that could
be repeated endlessly.*

1   Praise God your way,
         praise God my way.

2   God loves you.
God loves me.
God is love;
God is truth.
God has faith in us.
Thank you God.

1   Praise God...

PSALM 118:1–2, 14–24
The growth of confidence

1   God, you are good to us;
your love bursts the bounds of time.

2   You renew our confidence in you.

14   **With you beside us, we can face anything.**

15   We have no fears when you stand among us.

16   **A whisper races through your opponents' thoughts:**
"God has chosen a cause; no one can conquer God."

17   Winning or losing, living or dying, I want to be with God;
I want to celebrate God's goodness to me.

18   God has tested me. I have been through hell.
But God never abandoned me.

19   **Now I have the confidence to go anywhere,**
to try anything.

20   Whatever it takes, I know I'm worth it.

21   **Once, I had no confidence in myself,**
and I had no confidence in God.
I quivered with insecurities;
I was a raw wound, flinching from everything.

22   Now the fluff that drifted in the wind
has become a mighty cottonwood,
reaching high towards your smile.

23   **Only you could do this.**

24   A new day has dawned for me, a new life has begun.
Is it any wonder that I'm happy?

PSALM 118:1–2, 19–29
In times of terror

*Sometimes life is a bowl of cherries. Sometimes, it's more like a
trip to the emergency ward.*

1   As we ride the ambulance of life, Lord,
      facing endless uncertainties,
    we sense your presence beside us.

2   **Your constant love and care comforts us;**
      our fears fade away.

19   Where masked figures fix shattered souls,
      you hold my hand.

21   **In a time of terror, you hover over me;**
    you give me the breath of life.

22   **Vulnerability leaves us isolated and alone;**
      yet we are buoyed up by compassion.
    The moment we most fear becomes the moment to remember!

23   **This can only be God's grace.**

24   Awareness washes over us like returning consciousness.
    We are alive! We are not alone!

25   **Thank you, God. Thank you.**

26   Thank you for those who serve in your name.
    Our tears overflow with gratitude.

27   **God lives in the hearts and hands of healers.**
    Wherever there are people of goodwill,
    wherever kindness and compassion exist,
      God is.

28   **You are my God; I will thank you with every thought.**
    You are my God; I will honor you with all I do.

29   **I will never feel alone again;**
    in all the ambulances of life,
    your love will hold me up.

PSALM 118:14–24
God's rainbow

14 God's rainbow arches over me; I fear nothing any more.
15 For what can conquer God?
Before the beginning, and after the end,
God is, and God will be.
16 Everything works together for God's goals.
17 **If God is with me, nothing I do is wasted;**
like sunbeams dancing on a lake, even my weakest efforts
will gather into the glory of God.
18 **Gales may buffet me, and storm clouds may darken my face,**
but God will never give up on me.

19 I will arise and go now;
I will sink into God's watery womb,
20 **and rise again into a new life.**
A new day has dawned.
21 **God will look after me.**
22 As a piece of driftwood becomes a work of art,
so God will find new uses for me.

23 **Do not try to second-guess God,**
for God is greater than all our imaginings.
24 This is the day God gave us—
rejoice and be glad in it.

PSALM 118:19–29
Show us our doors

People who have recovered from near death experiences often
refer to moving towards a light.

19 Show us our doors, God,
so that we can step through them into new tomorrows.
Show us our opportunities, so that we can seize them!

20	God gives us many doors;
	we hold back instead of knocking boldly.
21	Knock, and the doors will be opened.
	Seek, and we will find the opportunities God offers us.
22, 23	Even a quivering coward can conquer new worlds.
24	**With God, we can fling our fears aside;**
	we can dance through every day.
25	**Show us our doors, God;**
	help us to recognize our opportunities.
26	**Open the door.**
	Happiness is yours in God's company.
	Those who live as God's companions welcome you.
27	**You will be surrounded by a swirl of light,**
	and pulled into the very pulse of God.
28	**You, God, you are my only God.**
	There is no other like you;
	I want nothing more than to be with you.
29	I will open your door;
	I will live in the light of your love forever.

PSALM 119:1–8
In good company

The original Psalm 119 is an enormously complex wordplay, to which I cannot possibly do justice in the few excerpts used by the lectionaries. So I chose to ignore the psalm's structure, and concentrate on its message.

1	How fortunate are those who have not fouled up their lives!
	They can hold their heads high in God's presence.
2	They are single-minded in pursuing God's way;
	They are not tempted to turn aside.

3   They try not to harm anyone;
                they follow the Lord's footsteps,
4   for God has shown us the way.

5   **God, help me to follow you faithfully.**
6   Let me keep my eyes fixed on your example,
                so that I do not disgrace myself;
7   **then my feet will not stumble,**
                and my stride will not slacken.
        I can come before you with a clean conscience.
8   I would like to walk with you, God; please walk with me.

PSALM 119:9–16
A better vision

9   The mass media paint pretty pictures
                of flaming passion and sensual pleasures.
                I will not deny it—they tempt me.
                Their insidious lies sneak under my skin—
                I have trouble telling right from wrong.
10   **Only your guidance, gathered through the generations,**
      keeps my feet from straying off the proven path.
                Your wisdom keeps my thoughts from wandering.
11   **I treasure each insight that you teach me.**
12   You are holy, God;
                infect me with your holiness.
                Make me more like what I was meant to be
                when you first conceived me.
13   **I can say all the right words**
                but still I am tempted.
14   I would rather hear you than the whispers of lust;
                turn my obsessions away from possessions.
15   Help me shut out the clamor of worldly wisdom;
                let me concentrate on you.
16   You are my guiding light, my model, my mentor.
                I will try to understand you;
                I will try to remember your wishes.

PSALM 119:33–40
Clear instructions

33   Give me your rules, your guides, your regulations,
and I will follow them all my life.
34 **Teach me your principles, so that I can understand your ways.**
35   I long for clear instructions;
I need each "i" dotted and each "t" crossed.
36   So point me in the right direction.
Put my life in order.
37   Don't let me be distracted by irrelevant details,
or drawn aside by passing fancies.
38   **Lay out your law, and let me follow it—**
I won't look for loopholes.
39   Do not treat me with contempt,
when I have pursued your policies without question.
40   **I don't believe in ad-libbing my way through life;**
I want a straight and narrow path that I can follow.

PSALM 119:97–104
The maze

97   In the maze of modern life, it helps to have clear directions.
98   **A clear vision of how things ought to be**
gives me a great advantage.
99   I don't have to balance this against that.
I don't constantly have to choose the lesser of two evils.
You give me a goal.
100   **The world is changing so fast,**
the wisdom of old age isn't always applicable;
but your wisdom is.
101   **Our ways are not always your ways,**
nor is our wisdom always your wisdom.
102   You have taught me how to discern the difference.
103   **And what a difference that makes!**
104   **You help me see more clearly;**
With your guidance, I can grope my way through.

PSALM 119:105–112
To mentors

All of us have had mentors, people who took us under their wing and helped us along.

105   You have been like a parent to me;
I have followed your advice faithfully.
106   I listen to your word.
I try to do your will.
107   But right now, my life is a mess.
I need your help.
108   Who else could I turn to?
Who else can I trust?
109   Like a billiard ball, I bounce from crisis to confrontation,
but still I try to measure up.
110   **The world tests me with temptations.**
They attract me, I cannot deny it;
But I do not give in.
111   I have learned well your precepts and principles;
they matter more to me than passing pleasures;
they are the foundation of my life.
112   I would yield only to one temptation,
the temptation to win your approval.

PSALM 119:129–136
Good advice

I have a sense, sometimes, that we only go to God when our lives fall apart, just as we only go to a golf pro when our game goes sour.

129   Lord, you've been around a lot longer than me,
so I listen to your advice.
130   **Your words are so wise**
that even a fool like me can understand them.

131   You speak, and I'm left open-mouthed;
I wonder why I hadn't thought of it myself.

132   Now I come to you again for help;
please be as patient as you have been in the past.
133   Keep me headed straight up the fairway.
Do not let me drift off into the rough.
134   I have had bad advice from others.
I need to get straightened out by an expert.
135   Only you can do it, God.
So smile on me, and show me your way.
136   I will be grateful forever.

PSALM 119:137–144
Persevering

*In any race, only one person can come first. We all like to win—
but failure is the more universal human experience.*

137   It is hard to serve you, God.
I cannot live up to your level of perfection.
138   Your standards are too high for me—
I can't measure up.
141a   I am only a frail and fallible human.
139   I do my best—
but often I feel like an outcast, an oddball;
hardly anyone recognizes what I'm trying to do.

140   I'm not asking for lower standards;
I know you are right.
Generations and generations have proved your rightness.
141b   I cannot ignore their insights.
142   **For you do not waver like a weather vane,
pointing whichever way the wind blows;**
popularity polls have no impact upon you.
Your values are eternal.

143   Although troubles swirl around me like autumn leaves,
still you show me the way.
144   **Your example is as dependable**
as a lighthouse in the darkness—
I can safely set my course by it.

PSALM 121
A hiker's creed

1   Somewhere out there, past the highest peaks,
someone watches over me.
2   **God made these peaks and these valleys,**
this air and this earth.
3   Yet God is close enough to guide my feet,
every step I take along life's precipitous paths.
4   **I may grow weary, but God does not nod off;**
my mind may wander, but God always stays alert.
5   **God watches over me.**

6   God stays as close to me
as the hat that shelters me from summer sun,
as close as the jacket
that shields me from the slashing rain.
God watches over me.
7 **God's hand holds me when I crawl along the edge of a cliff;**
it saves me from delusions of depending only on myself.
God keeps me from falling off the edge,
and keeps me safely on the path.
God watches over me.
8   **Wherever I go, wherever I may find myself,**
God will go with me and watch over me,
even into eternity.

PSALM 121
The closest companion

1   Let others seek their gods in the executive suite;
let them put their faith in rising to the top.

2   We know where our help comes from;
it comes from the one who made heaven and earth.

3, 5   Our God watches over every aspect of creation.
As a doting parent tends a toddler,
God holds out a hand when we stumble;
God will not let us fall down the stairs
before we have learned to walk on our own.

4   **God does not play off one person against another.**
God has no favorites;
God never tires of caring.

6   No crisis can destroy you;
though you lose loved ones, career, or health,

7   **if you retain your relationship with God,**
you will not be embittered;
you can emerge from the pain a better person.

8   **Wherever you go, whatever you do,**
God will go with you.

PSALM 122
The universal pilgrimage

*When does ecumenism become syncretism? I don't know. But I
have trouble believing that God is God only of those who wear
the right labels.*

1   God calls people everywhere to a pilgrimage.

2   **From all over the world,**
many feet beat a path to God's holy places.

3   They struggle over high mountain passes;
they shuffle across dusty deserts;
they crawl along the walls of river canyons.

4   **Straggling lines of searchers converge in a fertile valley;**
    a great shout of joy goes up to the heavens.
5   **Muslims, Christians, Jews, Hindus—in common cause**
    the great religions rise above doctrinal differences.

6   Pray for their unity;
                pray for their commitment.
7   May they not threaten each other;
        may they generate peace among their peoples.
8   God, watching over them, says,
        "They do not all call themselves my followers.
            Yet because they are brothers and sisters,
                    meeting in harmony,
                I will treat them as my own."
9   **Because they do God's will, God welcomes them.**

PSALM 123
Outside, looking in

*Anyone who feels excluded, shut out, treated as inferior, might
sympathize with this psalm.*

1   I wish I were like you.
        You have so much more than we have;
        you are so much more than we are.
2   You are the norm, the model, the image everyone expects of us.
            We discern you at a distance,
        as through the wrong end of a telescope.
            You are out of reach, untouchable.

3   **Please don't ignore us.**
    We have had more than our share of contempt dumped on us.
4   **For too long, we have been the rejects,**
            the people nobody cares about.

PSALM 124
The only explanation

*Does God intervene in human affairs? Sometimes that seems like
the only explanation that makes any sense. In those situations,
it's hard not to sound excessively exultant.*

1   We must have had God's help.
    The odds were all against us.
2   If we had not had right and justice on our side,
3   our opponents would have destroyed us.
4   **We would have burst like balloons;**
    we would have plummeted in the popularity polls.
5   **But that didn't happen.**
6   We must have had God's help;
    no one else could have done it.
7   We evaded the trap the other side set for us.
    Now their scheming has been exposed;
    no one will trust them any more.
8   We must have had God's help.
    There is no other explanation.

PSALM 125
Let there be fairness

*The vision of the psalms does not always correspond to harsh
reality—but it is worth wishing for.*

1   Mountains are not easily moved.
    God's people have faith like that.
2   As mountains gather around a little town,
    cradling it in the hollow of their valleys,
    so God wraps loving arms around her children,
    to protect them from abuse and exploitation.
3   Hands of hate shall not touch them;
    no guns or war toys will fall into their cribs.

They will not be tempted by violence later in life;
they will have no desire to make victims of others.

4   Let it be so, Lord.
           Let it be so.
Let a good start lead to goodness as an adult.
Show us that there is an innate fairness in the universe.
5   **Let those who turn away from you,**
     who prefer their own ways to yours,
     fade out of the limelight.
Those who follow your way do not expect fame or fortune;
but let there be fairness.

PSALM 126
Harvest thanksgiving

*The psalm writers were a pastoral people, depending on
agriculture for their survival. Simply being spared a disaster
was cause for celebration.*

1   God has been good to us.
The storm clouds gathered, the hail hung overhead—
but it passed by.
2   Then we laughed and danced;
our peals of joy echoed across our lands.
Celebration spread faster than fire through autumn grass,
faster than rumors on a summer night.
3   For God has done great things for us.
We are overcome with gratitude.

4   The desert is not kind, oh God.
It demands living on the edge of disaster.
Give us some sparkling springs!
5   **We watered the desert with our tears;**
     with our hearts in our mouths,
     we watched the green shoots stretch up.

6   **We risked everything on the seeds we planted;**
we sank our lives into this soil.
Now the harvest has come home a hundredfold.
God, you have renewed our lives.

PSALM 126
Second spring

There are many kinds of prisons.

1   When the gates of our prisons opened,
we could not believe it.
2   **Stone walls sank behind us;**
the sky opened above us;
we did cartwheels for joy.
Those who gathered to celebrate our release
said to themselves, "God has been good to them."
3   **Indeed, we could not have set ourselves free;**
God must have had a hand in it.

4   **Now we must rebuild our broken lives,**
like piecing together shards of shattered pottery.
5   May we find as much joy in putting the pieces together
as we had sorrow in their shattering.
6   **These new lives were born in pain and suffering;**
with God's help, they can still blossom
into a second spring.

PSALM 126
New horizons

This paraphrase is for all new beginnings—but perhaps especially for men and women breaking out of the Ken-and-Barbie mentality.

1   The truth dawns on us—
we are appalled at what we have been.
For too long we have been captives of our self-image;
for too long we have let ourselves live a lie.
2   At last we are free!
Instead of narrow roles, we can see new horizons!
Our chains have fallen off—
we can move freely once more.

Behind their bars, some still shake their heads,
but those who preceded us into freedom weep tears of joy.
3   **This change could not come**
through our individual insights;
God must have had a hand in it.

4   **But now we are unsure, Lord.**
The uncharted wilderness of our new world
stretches before us;
we no longer know which way to turn.
5   Fearful of falling, we take tentative steps.
We would love to run effortlessly.
6   We have thrown away so many opportunities;
there is so little time left.

For this chance to start again, Lord, we thank you.

PSALM 127
The best insurance

In the wisdom of the psalmist's time, children offered the only social security most families had. An abundance of children was a blessing. Today, we are blessed with many more ways of providing for help in time of trouble.

1 The road of life takes many tricky turns;
you never know what crisis waits around the corner.
2 Each day has only 24 hours.
You cannot accomplish any more
by burning candles at both ends;
you will only burn yourself out.
3 **But gather friends and goodwill as you go,**
and you will never lack strength for your tasks.
4 A surplus of goodwill pays off better than any insurance policy.
5 **Treat everyone as a friend,**
and you will never lack support for your journey.

PSALM 128
The lingering gift

The psalms sometimes sound idealistic, utopian. But at certain times and passages of our life—at weddings, for example—that's just how we feel.

1 Joy belongs to those who belong to the Lord,
to those who live in harmony with God.

2 **The gardens you tend will grow lush with life;**
they will feed you richly;
you will count yourself fortunate.
3 **Your family will grow like shoots in springtime.**
They will grow tall and straight, holding their heads high.
Through all your days, your partner will spread peace ·
like dew on a summer morn.

4   Your days will be filled with sunshine if you love the Lord.
5   **May God bless you;**
        may your good fortune rub off on everyone you meet,
6   so that your distant descendants
                recognize the legacy you left them,
                    the lingering gift of goodwill.

1   **Joy belongs to those who belong to the Lord,**
            to those who live in harmony with God.

PSALM 130
The pit

A patient described clinical depression as a deep black pit with
shiny walls too smooth to climb. (As an editor, I suspect a later
author of tacking on "the moral" in verses 7-8.)

1   From the bottom of a deep black pit, God, I scream at you.
2   **The walls rise above my head, shutting out the sun.**
                Can you hear me, God?
            I can't get out by my own efforts.
3   I've tried and tried.
                I climb part way out,
            and then I slide back again to the bottom.
                Without your help, I'm sunk forever.
4   **Don't judge me—forgive me!**
                Free me from my secret faults.
                Give me another chance!
5   **I shall lie down here in the depths of the pit and wait.**
                You are my only hope.
6   **I shall wait for your response.**
                I know I will not be disappointed.

7   **Put your hope in the Lord.**
            You will not be disappointed either.
8   God can free us from our failures,
                and save us from our successes.

PSALM 131:1–3
Ordinary people

For homemakers and secretaries and other people who are too often overlooked.

2   I take care of little things.
              I keep life running smoothly.
1   **I do not want to seem proud or ambitious.**
           I keep my eyes on the ground;
           I don't push my own views;
      I don't meddle with business or politics.
2   But I take care of little things.
              I keep life running smoothly.
I have learned to be content, not to be brazen or demanding;
    I accept whatever life brings me with humility.
3   **Is there hope for people like me, too, Lord?**
    Does glory go only to the great and the mighty?
2   I take care of little things.
              I keep life running smoothly.

PSALM 132:1–10
Lament of an aging congregation

David thought that one temple would be sufficient to house the Lord. He would be amazed to see churches sprouting like dandelions in every town and city—and each one precious to its people.

1   With bake sales and bazaars beyond number, Lord,
           we raised the funds for this building.
2   **We held strawberry socials and silent auctions;**
           we raided piggy banks and cashed in savings bonds.
4   **We could not sleep, worrying about our mortgage.**
3   At home, at work, at play, we thought of little else.
5   **We wanted this church!**
          We needed this church!
      We were going to build this church!

6　　The word of our commitment got around.
**People came out of the community
like blackbirds popping from a pie.**
7　　They pitched in at potluck suppers
and hammered nails in building bees.
They joined committees and shared in worship.
8　　It was a great time, God.
When it was finished, we held our heads high.
We flung open the door to invite you in,
9　　and found you were already there.

10　　**We are growing old and tired now, God.
Don't leave us because we lack the energy we once had.**
Don't let our church close
because disillusioned people drift away to other challenges.
11　　**You promised to be with us, always.**
12　　Don't let our church die.

PSALM 132:11–17
The tree of life

11　　When God makes a promise,
**God does not break it.
So God said:**
"I have chosen to live with you.
I will live with your children, too,
12　　**if they continue faithful.**
If they abide by our agreement,
then their children, and their children's children,
will also enjoy my company."

13　　**God made a choice;**
God chose to be part of this people, this planet.
14　　God said,
**"This is my home.
I will be life itself.**

15   As long as I live here,
life on earth will be rich and abundant.
16   **I will be as close as their clothing
to those who do not vandalize my artistry,**
as close as their skin
to all living things that remain true to my vision.
17   **Do not look to outsiders to rescue the earth;**
the tree of life has its roots right here."

PSALM 133
Family reunion

We don't pour oil over people's heads any more. But the image of a gathered people, of good things overflowing, still has meaning.

1   How good it feels to have the human family
gathered together for this sumptuous feast.
2   **Here we rejoice in the rich repast
of fruit and tree and vine.**
Apples and oranges, grapes and cherries,
yield their joyous juices to our lusting mouths.
**Drops of surplus pleasure trickle down our chins.
We dab them unself-consciously with rumpled napkins.**
3 This gathering refreshes like a sweet morning in the mountains,
like a prairie sky polished bright by gentle breezes.
**Surely this is what the Lord intended
when God created life.**

PSALM 133
Life partners

Dedicated to all couples whose marriages have survived the traumas of growing up.

1   You have grown from my lover to my best friend,
my closest companion.

2   **You know me better than I know myself;**
your company is as comforting as a deep warm bath.
The sweet oil of your presence
softens the knots of my tangled emotions.
3   Every morning I wake,
wondering what I did to deserve you;
every night, I sleep
with the blessing of your breath beside me.

PSALM 135:1–14
To the team captain

On a school playground, it was always agony, waiting to be picked for a team, hoping to avoid the humiliation of being left to the last.

1   Choose me, God, choose me!
2   **From the crowds standing around, choose me now.**
3   I want to play on your team.
I want to be on the winning side.

4   Oh, thank you, God, thank you.
I won't let you down, I promise.
5   You are my captain.
You are the best of all.
6   Whatever you turn your hand to, you do well.
7   **I think you're wonderful.**
The sun rises and sets on you.
8, 10   **No one else stands a chance against you,**
11   **no matter how high and mighty they think they are.**
9   If they knew what they were up against,
they would quit right now.
12   **I want to win with you.**
13   Someday, they'll engrave your name on a cup;
they'll enshrine your jersey in the Hall of Fame.

14   Then I can claim my small share in your glory.

PSALM 136:1–9, 23–26
God's love lasts forever

1   At the beginning of the beginning, God loved.
At the end of the end, God will still be loving.
God's love lasts forever.

2   Many gods are worshiped every day,
in temples of commerce and conflict.
But God's love lasts forever.

3   Other gods will come into favor and fade away;
they will fall in and out of fashion.
But God's love lasts forever.

4   Systems and authorities grow and fade;
they have their own devotees and disciples.
But God's love lasts forever.

5, 6   Other gods claim to manage the sea and sky,
the earth and its fullness.
Only God can claim to have created them.
For God's love lasts forever.

7–9   Science says that even the sun is not eternal;
it will consume the solar system in a shell of fire.
But God's love lasts forever.

23   Other gods favor the rich and the powerful;
they ignore those who don't know the right buttons to push.
But God's love lasts forever.

24   But God watches over the forgotten creatures;
no refugee or fruit fly is overlooked.
God's love lasts forever.

25, 26   God is one with those who suffer;
God is one with all creation.
God's love lasts forever.

1   At the beginning of the beginning, God loved.
At the end of the end, God will still be loving.

PSALM 137:1–6
Yearning for home

An immigrant is also an emigrant, often feeling exiled, often grieving. To begin a new life means leaving behind a familiar life.

1   Where the willows drape over the weedy water's edge,
        we weep.
    We remember our own rivers—
    icy rapids racing among the rocks.
2   Beneath the arching branches,
    our tears trickle down onto muddy banks.

3   **The people here say we should be happy;**
    they want us to wear permanent smiles.
    "Do another of your ethnic dances," they call;
    "Entertain us with the riches of your race, your religion!"
4   How can we dance with our feet mired in mud?
5   **Removed from our familiar rocks,**
    our hearts rot within us.

6   My spirit has been siphoned out of me;
    our dreams drain away.
    I cannot reject my roots so easily;
    I cannot pretend to belong to this place.

PSALM 138
Humble and lowly

In biblical times, worshipers prostrated themselves on the ground before the Holy of Holies, while reciting this psalm. For us, it's a strange position from which to express gratitude.

1   This is your home, your turf, your territory.
    I am so glad to be here
    that I kiss the earth you walk on.

2   I fling myself into the dust,
the floor of your dwelling.
I extend my arms to embrace your earth.

But you lift me up from my lowly position.
You take me up as your guest.
You make me one of your family;
you even give me your name!
3   You take me under your wing.
When I cry out, you cover me;
I benefit from your strength.

4   Foxes may lord it over the chicken coop,
and squirrels over the sparrow's nest,
but no creatures challenge the eagle's rule.
5   **As the eagle soars above the fieldmice,**
so do you, Lord, rise above us mortals.
6   Daily duties keep us scurrying close to the earth.
But you watch over us from on high;
you can see danger long before it draws near.
7   **Troubles grow around us like tall grass**
but in the shadow of your outspread pinions,
predators scatter like minnows.
8   **You watch over me,**
because you have a place for me in your plans.

PSALM 139:1–12, 23–24
Transparent to God

1   I am transparent to you, God.
You can see right through me.
2   I can hide nothing from you.
You read my body language,
and detect my deepest feelings.
3   The tiniest quirks of my handwriting
reveal everything going on inside me.

4   You know what I'm going to say
           before I've thought it through.
5   I look around at the world, and you are there;
           I look within my psyche, and you are there;
           emotion and intellect are one to you.
6   You know me better than I know myself.
           I could not stand knowing myself that well—
           I need some hidden corners still to discover,
           some mysteries still to unfold.
7   Only you can cope with total knowledge.

7   How can I have a life of my own?
8   If I study science, you are there.
           If I explore economics, you are there.
9   From charmed quarks to exploding galaxies,
           from icebergs to dinosaurs to industrial toxins—
           wherever I turn, you will turn up too.
           You insinuate yourself into every crevice of my life.
11   Even if I bury myself in my work, you break in,
           and upset all my careful applecarts.
10   You drag me forward by my lapels;
           in the small of my back, you keep shoving me.
12   I cannot keep you out of my life.
           You are my permanent partner.

23   I have nothing to hide from you.
           Go ahead—look into my soul!
24   Clean out any festering sores;
           make me fit to share life completely with you.

PSALM 139:13–18
Inescapable God

13   No wonder you know me so well, God.
           Before my mother knew I existed,
           you wrote the genetic code of my cells.
14   You created my life.

15   **Wombs and worlds are one to you;**
they have no secrets from you;
you are the essence of all life.

16   As once you shaped the cells
that formed my fingernails and my hair,
so still you guide me through each day.

17   Even if I am only a fleeting thought
flickering through your mind,
I am in good company.

18   **All of creation owes its existence to you, God.**
I can no more imagine your thoughts
than I can recall every detail of my dreams.
But you are not a dream,
for when I wake, you are still with me.

PSALM 143:1–8
Out in the cold

More and more people find themselves laid off in the prime of life. Their sense of worth vanishes with their job.

1   Listen to my misery, Lord.
Lend an ear to my lonely plea;
don't pass me by; be kind to me.

2   **Don't make me defend my appeal to you.**
I don't deserve your consideration—no one does.

3   **I can't stand on my own any more.**
Life has ground me down;
I am a pile of dust, swept into the corner by a new broom.

4   I've been cast aside,
pitched onto the trash pile.
I feel useless, worthless, helpless.

5   But it wasn't always like this.
Once upon a time, I was your favored friend.
You carried me on your shoulders.

6   **Do it again, Lord.**
     I'm begging you.
7   But do it soon, Lord.
     I'm fading fast.
     Don't wash your hands of me,
     or I will go down the drain.
8   Let me wake up tomorrow to your love;
     let me fall asleep tonight with your arms around me.
     Give me your hand, and lead me through my life.
     For you are my reason for living.

PSALM 143:1–8
Cry myself to sleep

A best friend finds another best friend; a lover leaves; a marriage breaks up. Everyone knows that feeling of being abandoned.

1   I sit by the telephone,
     waiting for you to return my calls.
2   **This is no way to treat your friends, God.**
     Yes, I have disappointed you.
     But who hasn't?
3   **We are only human, after all.**
     Only you are divine.
4   **I cannot try any harder. I despair.**
5   I remember how things used to be.
     I remember how close we were, once.
6   I reach out for you,
     but my groping hand touches only empty space.
7   **Where are you, God?**
     Why have you forsaken me?
8   **At night, I cry myself to sleep.**
     I dream that when I wake, you will be there again.
     You are my life.

PSALM 145:1–9
Bubbling joy

Some psalms do nothing more—as if that weren't enough!—than praise God.

1   Blue skies again this morning, God.
2   It's almost too good to be true.
            Each day takes my breath away—
            it is beautiful beyond belief.
3   And you made it all.
4   **Words fail me.**
            Everything I try to say comes out in superlatives.
            I wish I could express my feelings.
5   You are never out of my thoughts;
            I'm conscious of you every waking moment.
6   You ride beside me on the roads;
            you sit next to me at my desk;
            you touch my sleeve in the shopping mall.
7   **If only I could show others your presence**
            as clearly as I see it myself.
            Then they could share
            this wonderful bubbling of joy inside.

8   **For you are wonderful to know, God.**
            You are gracious and merciful;
            you have a quick smile and a long fuse.
9   **You love everything that you have made,**
            and you made everything.

PSALM 145:8–13
No favored nation clause

Maybe every part of creation is special to God, and not just humans.

8   God is generous and just;
No part of creation gets special treatment.
God does not favor one creature over another,
but treats all with equal care.
9   God's overflowing love pours out
to all creatures, great and small;
God cares for sand and for stars,
for humus and for humans.

10   All your works witness to your wonders, oh God.
In you, everything works together for good.
11   They gather into a great glory;
they reveal the rightness of your rule.
12   If only we could open our eyes,
we could see how lions and lambs, herons and humans,
each have a right to be here.
13   **For your realm supersedes time and space;**
boundaries and jurisdictions mean nothing to you.
Your presence permeates everything—
From before the beginning to beyond the end.

PSALM 145:13b–21
More than mortals

13   Governments come, and governments go;
nations come, and nations go.
Only God goes on forever.
Only God is completely dependable,
never corrupted by power.
14   God strengthens those crushed by life,
and lifts the burdens of those bent over by cares.

15 **God does not favor the fortunate;**
the seasons roll around for the poor as for the rich.
16 **With open-handed generosity,**
God causes the earth to bring forth food for all.
17 Only humans hoard, creating shortages for others.
But God holds nothing back;
God plays fair with everyone.
18 **God never puts the phone on hold**
or hides behind secretaries or schedules.
God is always available.
19 **God turns no one away—**
20 **except those who deny the existence of God.**
When their time comes, they will vanish into silence;
their story will be heard no more.
21 But the stories of those who know God
will be told down the generations;
by their stories, many not yet born will come to know God.

PSALM 146
The test for God's way

1 Who can you trust these days?
Only God. Forever and ever.
2 You can put your faith in God as long as you live.
God will never let you down.
3 Do not put your trust only in governments.
They come and they go.
4 **Human life is short, but governments are shorter.**
With each election, their policies change;
their promises dry up faster than morning dew.
5 Put your trust in God;
for eternal confidence,
count on the one who knows eternity.
6 What human agency can claim to have created the earth?
What human agency can claim to care for it?
7 **Look and see those whom God chooses to help:**
to feed the hungry; to set free the prisoners;

8   to give sight to the blind; to let the lame walk;
to grant liberty to the oppressed...
9   **Those who always take care of themselves first
are left to the last.**
God cares for the strangers, the widows, the orphans—
**God watches over those
who cannot watch out for themselves.**
10   Can any human authority make that claim?
That is why God rules over all creation.
Trust in God forever!

PSALM 146:5–10
God keeps faith with us

5   Put your faith in God.
6   **God made heaven and earth,
the sea, the sky, and the continents.**
God made everything that lives in the waters,
that walks on the earth, that flies in the skies.
God keeps faith with them all.
Surely God will do the same for you.
7   **God's spirit proclaims good news to the poor,
release to the captives,
recovery of sight to the blind.**
8   God's holy spirit lifts up those
who are bent over with responsibilities,
who are burdened with the struggle to do right.
9   **God does not protect only good solid citizens.**
God looks after transients, immigrants, and gays,
illegitimate children, and single mothers.
10   **God will not break faith.
Not now. Not ever.**
Thank God for that!

PSALM 147:2–11
Not impressed by appearances

2   We are the refugees.
Our homes and our spirits have been destroyed.
Across the earth we have fled seeking asylum.
God gathered us together, and gave us a second chance.

3   We are the sick, the infirm, the elderly.
God gave us nurses, and medicines,
and medicare to cover the costs that would have crushed us.

4   We are the students, the scientists, the scholars.
The more we explore our universe,
the more the mysteries we encounter fill us with awe.

6   We are the poor, the oppressed,
the people at the bottom of the pile.
We see the powerful and mighty come tumbling down,
betrayed by their own corruption.

5   How can you see all this, and doubt the power of God?
8   **If God can make the rain fall, the grass grow,**
the rivers run, and the sun shine,
9   **if God can balance the needs of nature**
so that both lion and lamb can live,
then surely God can also affect human affairs.

10   We are not well-dressed, or privileged;
we are not wealthy or important.
But God does not judge by appearances.
God is not impressed by titles and positions,
nor influenced by body-building and cosmetic beauty.
In the eyes of God, a pauper matters as much as a priest,
a person on welfare as much as a president.
11   What matters is how well we hear God,
and how much we care for each other.

178   **James Taylor**

PSALM 147:12–20
God does things differently

12 God does things differently.

13 **By the wisdom of this world,**
an unborn child has no value.
It has no name; it is not yet a person.
Yet while it is still in the womb,
it somersaults with joy.

14 Its mother's eyes shine with hope;
her breasts swell in preparation for the milk of life.

15 To the mother, the unborn child within matters
more than any international agreement;
she wraps it in her own body.

16 God carries us in her womb.
With her own lifeblood, God feeds us.
Like mother preparing a nursery for her newborn,
God readies the earth to receive us.

17 **Winter gives way to spring;**
frozen hearts thaw;
tightly buttoned spirits open to warmth.

18 That is God's way:
out of darkness comes light;
out of ice, water;
out of pain and struggle, new life.

19 That is how God gives birth.

20 **Others may not recognize this mystery.**
But to us God has revealed the miracle.
Our cry of weakness is a cry of triumph;
our thirst invites us to lie close to the heart of God
and drink our fill.

God does things differently. Thank God.

PSALM 148
Salute to the new year

The shortest day of the year has passed; the days grow longer again.

1   Come join the joyful dance of life!
             Celebrate each moment of increasing light!
2   When the sun comes out after the snow,
             when the south wind blows the blizzards away,
             all of creation creeps out of its caves
             to soak up the welcome warmth.
3   **All things bright and beautiful,**
             all creatures great and small,
4   **all things wise and wonderful...**
5   the Lord God made them all.

6   **God created their characteristics and personalities;**
8   the rain falls, the wind blows,
             the frost forms its delicate traceries, all as they should.
             Rain does not rise, nor frost burst into flames—
             they know their form and function;
             the Lord God made them all.

7   **So join the joyful dance of life.**
             The silvery fish can shiver and shimmy;
9   **peaks and ridges march in royal ranks;**
             trees can wave and grasses weave;
10   **cattle can stomp and marmots whistle,**
             chicks can cheep and porcupines bristle;
             the Lord God made them all.

11, 12   **The planet throbs with the pulse of life;**
             heartbeats pound their passionate rhythm.
             Princes and popes, outlaws and outcasts,
             all races, all colors, all ages, all species,
             swirl like galaxies glowing in a summer night.
             The Lord God made them all.

13 **There are no wallflowers in God's great dance;**
each piece of creation has its own part to play.
14 **We humans live and die;**
our communities come and go,
our empires rise and fall;
the Lord God made them all...

And the dance goes on.

PSALM 148
Profligate generosity

1 Jubilation, exaltation, celebration, one and all!
2 **Within the womb of the heavens,**
the earth leaps to praise its Creator.
3, 4 As the pearl necklace of planets swings around the sun,
as the shining oceans embrace the continents,
so do all living things praise the giver of life.
5 **For God expressed a thought, and the thought took life.**
6 God wanted to speak,
and the Word became flesh and lived among us.
7 **In that Word was holiness,**
the spirit that makes every life
more than the sum of its chemicals.
From the tiniest plankton in the sea to the great whales,
from the ants that burrow in the dust
to the eagle that soars in the heavens—
all owe their existence to God.

8 **Fire and hail, snow and frost,**
sun and drought, wind and rain—
in God, all things work together for good.
9 Mighty mountains compost into rich soil;
fruit trees and cedars aerate the atmosphere.
10 The dung beetle depends on the wastes of cattle;
birds and currents carry seeds to new orchards.

11   No one is cut off from God's energy,
neither presidents throned in offices
nor derelicts huddled under bridges.

12   For in God there is neither male nor female,
old nor young, black nor white.

13   **All have been equally created by God;**
their lives all witness to God's grace.

14   **With profligate generosity,**
God scatters new life among weeds and thistles.
And all of creation responds with rejoicing.

PSALM 149
The communion of saints

In recent years, many autocratic governments have been overthrown—not by force or power, but by the accumulative energy of ordinary people, the communion of saints.

1   Familiar words aren't enough.
New times call for new ways to praise God.

2   So dance. Sing. Do something!
Show you love God with your bodies as well as your words.

3   Use every means you have
—your music, your work, your social systems—
to demonstrate your love for God.

4   **God will not shun you because you show your emotions.**
Love is not limited to important positions or plummy accents.

5   So join together with others.
Link your hands and link your lives.
Clap your hands and sing;
raise the roof in praise of God.

6   Let the vigor of your voices overflow into your living.
Seize each challenge as an opportunity

7   **to promote justice among all the people,**
to bring to judgment those who cause pain and suffering.

8   **Even ruthless dictators cannot resist**
     the surge of popular pressure.
     The longer they try to withstand the tide,
          the deeper they drown.
9   **That is how to give God praise.**
     Let us praise God!

PSALM 150
God's playground

A jam session is a good image of praise. So is a playground.

1   God has given us a glorious playground;
          let us have fun together!
2   **Climb to the top of the stairs**
     with your heart in your mouth;
     slide down the shiny slope with shrieks of glee.
3   Ride the swings higher and higher
     until you can reach out and touch the sky;
     swirl around on the merry-go-round
     until your head swims.
4   Build dream castles in the sandbox;
     bounce on the trampoline
     and soar above your troubles.
5   Chase your friends in a game of tag;
     throw your arms around everyone in a giant hug.

6   Let our games, our imaginings, our activities,
     announce to all that this is God's playground.
     God gave it to us to enjoy together.
     Come! Praise God in God's playground!

INDEX (BY THEME)

Good intentions
Ps 101

Gratitude: see Thankfulness

Grief
Ps 137:1-6

Growth
Ps 66:10-20; Ps 68:5-10, 32-35;
Ps 80:1-7, 17-19

Guidance
Ps 25:1-10; Ps 119:129-136

Happiness: see Joy

Harmony
Ps 19; Ps 27:1, 4-9; Ps 36:5-10;
Ps 122; Ps 19:7-14

Healing
Ps 51; Ps 107:1-3, 17-22; Ps 107:1-9;
Ps 107:23-32; Ps 118:1-2, 19-29;
Ps 118:19-29

Holiness
Ps 34:9-14; Ps 63:1-8; Ps 93; Ps 99

Hope
Ps 27:7-14; Ps 72:1-7, 10-14;
Ps 78:12-16; Ps 103:1-13; Ps 128;
Ps 132:1-10

Hospitality
Ps 15; Ps 36:5-10

Humility
Ps 65; Ps 99; Ps 104:1-9; Ps 106:1-15,
19-22, 23; Ps 131; Ps 139:1-12

Idealism
Ps 72:1-7, 10-14; Ps 107:33-38, 43;
Ps 110; Ps 128

Intervention
Ps 44:1-8; Ps 66:1-9; Ps 124

Intimacy
Ps 139:1-12, 23-24; Ps 139:13-18

Joy
Ps 40:1-11; Ps 96; Ps 100; Ps 126;
Ps 135:1-14; Ps 145:1-8; Ps 150

Judgment
Ps 2; Ps 9:9-20; Ps 33:10-22; Ps 41; Ps
50; Ps 52; Ps 53; Ps 73; Ps 82;
Ps 95:8-11

Justice
Ps 73; Ps 82; Ps 85:1-2, 8-13;
Ps 107:1-3, 17-22; Ps 145:8-13;
Ps 147:1-11

Laws
Ps 19; Ps 115:1-18; Ps 119:33-40;
Ps 119:105-112;

Leadership
Ps 72:1-7, 10-14

Learning
Ps 19; Ps 94:12-22

Liberation
Ps 30; Ps 78:12-16; Ps 126

Loneliness
Ps 4; Ps 10; Ps 22; Ps 63:1-8;
Ps 72:7-14; Ps 80:8-18; Ps 102:1-12

Loss
Ps 27:7-14; Ps 137:1-6

Love
Ps 20; Ps 22:23-31; Ps 84; Ps 114;
Ps 115:1-18; Ps 116:1-2, 12-19

Loyalty
Ps 26; Ps 119:1-8

Mortality
Ps 16; Ps 49; Ps 90:1-12

Nature
Ps 19:7-14; Ps 24; Ps 84:1-7;
Ps 92:1-4, 12-15; Ps 95; Ps 132:11-18

New life
Ps 30; Ps 40:1-11; Ps 51; Ps 80:1-7,
17-19; Ps 107:23-32; Ps 114; Ps 126;
Ps 147:12-20; Ps 148

Obedience
Ps 1

Peace
Ps 27:1, 4-9; Ps 36:5-10; Ps 46; Ps 97

Persistence
Ps 76; Ps 77:1-2, 11-20; Ps 139:1-12,
23-24

Pilgrimage
Ps 122

Pity: see Rescue

Praise
Ps 8; Ps 22:25-31; Ps 24; Ps 33:1-9; Ps
47; Ps 48; Ps 67; Ps 68:5-10, 32-35; Ps
76; Ps 84:1-7; Ps 93; Ps 103:19-22; Ps
105:1-6; Ps 111; Ps 117; Ps 121;
Ps 135:1-14; Ps 136:1-9, 23-26; Ps 138

Protection
Ps 3; Ps 28; Ps 29; Ps 121
see also Caring

Reassurance
Ps 1; Ps 4; Ps 23; Ps 97; Ps 104:14-18;
Ps 118:1-2, 19-29; Ps 118:19-29

Rejection
Ps 26; Ps 57:1-5; Ps 69:7-18; Ps 70; Ps
123

Rejoicing
Ps 118:14-24 see also Joy

Relief
Ps 27:1-6

Rescue
Ps 3; Ps 10:12-18; Ps 27:1, 4-9; Ps
31:1-5, 15-16; Ps 40:1-11; Ps 44:1-8; Ps
57:6-11; Ps 66:1-9; Ps 71:1-6;
Ps 78:23-29; Ps 78:34-38; Ps 86:1-10,
16-17; Ps 90:13-17; Ps 116:1-4, 12-19;
Ps 116:1-9

Responsibility
Ps 33:10-22; Ps 76; Ps 89:20-37;
Ps 111; Ps 112:1-9; Ps 131

Risk
Ps 31:1-5, 15-16; Ps 91:1-6

Roots
Ps 78:1-7

Sacrifice
Ps 22:23-31

Science
Ps 19:1-6; Ps 19:7-14

Shelter
Ps 28

Sickness
Ps 13

Stillness
Ps 46

Struggle
Ps 42; Ps 46

Success
Ps 45; Ps 49; Ps 73

Suffering
Ps 13; Ps 22; Ps 31:9-16; Ps 35:17-28;
Ps 54; Ps 69:7-18; Ps 70; Ps 79:1-9; Ps
86:1-10, 16-17; Ps 102:1-12;
Ps 130; Ps 143:1-8; Ps 147:12-20

Temptation
Ps 45; Ps 119:9-16

Thankfulness
Ps 65; Ps 67; Ps 68:5-10, 32-35;
Ps 95:1-7; Ps 96; Ps 113; Ps 116:1-4,
12-19; Ps 118:1-2, 14-24; Ps 118:14-24;
Ps 119:105-112; Ps 126; Ps 145:1-8;
Ps 149

Togetherness: see Family, Friendship

Trust
Ps 14; Ps 21:1-7; Ps 29; Ps 31:1-5,
15-16; Ps 31:9-16; Ps 31:19-24;
Ps 33:18-22; Ps 45; Ps 66:10-20;
Ps 71:1-6; Ps 72:7-14; Ps 91:9-16;
Ps 145:13b-21; Ps 146

Vengeance
Ps 2; Ps 3; Ps 9:9-20; Ps 10;
Ps 35:17-28

Victory
Ps 44:1-8; Ps 124

Violence
Ps 79:1-9
Vision
Ps 89:20-37; Ps 119:97-104

Waiting: see Expectation, Hope

Welcome
Ps 15 see also Hospitality

Wisdom
Ps 19:7-14; Ps 34:9-14; Ps 49; Ps 73;
Ps 78:1-7; Ps 119:97-104; Ps 127;
Ps 147:1-11

Yearning
Ps 42; Ps 80:8-18

INDEX (BY SUNDAY)

Day	Psalm	Lect.	Day	Psalm	Lect.
Easter Vigil	Ps 136:1-9, 23-26	R	Jun 26-Jul 2	Ps 13	R
Easter Vigil	Ps 16	R, C	Jun 26-Jul 2	Ps 89:1-4, 15-18	R
Easter Vigil	Ps 19	R, C	Jun 26-Jul 2	Ps 17:1-7, 15	C
Easter Vigil	Ps 30	C	Jul 3-9	Ps 45:10-17	R
Easter Vigil	Ps 33	C	Jul 3-9	Ps 145:8-14	R
Easter Vigil	Ps 42	R, C	Jul 3-9	Ps 124	C
Easter Vigil	Ps 43	R	Jul 10-16	Ps 119:105-112	R
Easter Vigil	Ps 46	R, C	Jul 10-16	Ps 65:(1-8), 9-13	R
Easter Vigil	Ps 98	R, C	Jul 10-16	Ps 69:6-15	C
Easter Vigil	Ps 143	R, C	Jul 17-23	Ps 139:1-12, 23-24	R
Easter Vigil	Ps 114	R, C	Jul 17-23	Ps 86:11-17	R
Easter	Ps 118:1-2, 14-24	R	Jul 17-23	Ps 103:1-13	C
			Jul 24-30	Ps 105:1-11, 45b	R
Easter	Ps 118:14-24	C	Jul 24-30	Ps 128	R
Easter 2	Ps 16	R	Jul 24-30	Ps 119:129-136	R
Easter 2	Ps 16:5-11	C	Jul 24-30	Ps 105:1-11	C
Easter 3	Ps 116:1-4, 12-19	R	Jul 31-Aug 6	Ps 17:1-7, 15	R
			Jul 31-Aug 6	Ps 145:8-9, 14-21	R
Easter 3	Ps 116:12-19	C	Jul 31-Aug 6	Ps 143:1-10	C
Easter 4	Ps 23	R, C	Aug 7-13	Ps 105:1-6, 16-22, 45b	R
Easter 5	Ps 31:1-5, 15-16	R	Aug 7-13	Ps 85:8-13	R
Easter 5	Ps 31:1-8	C	Aug 7-13	Ps 106:4-12	C
Easter 6	Ps 66:8-20	R, C	Aug 14-20	Ps 133	R
Ascension	Ps 47	R, C	Aug 14-20	Ps 67	R
Ascension	Ps 93	R	Aug 14-20	Ps 78:1-3, 10-20	C
Easter 7	Ps 68:1-10, 32-35	R	Aug 21-27	Ps 124	R
Easter 7	Ps 68:1-10	C	Aug 21-27	Ps 138	R
Pentecost	Ps 104:24-34, 35b	R	Aug 21-27	Ps 95	C
Pentecost	Ps 104:24-34	C	Aug 28-Sep 3	Ps 105:1-6, 23-26, 45c	R
Trinity Sunday	Ps 8	R	Aug 28-Sep 3	Ps 26:1-8	R
Trinity Sunday	Ps 33:1-12	C	Aug 28-Sep 3	Ps 114	C
May 29-Jun 4	Ps 46	R	Sep 4-10	Ps 149	R
May 29-Jun 4	Ps 31:1-5, 19-24	R	Sep 4-10	Ps 119:33-40	R
May 29-Jun 4	Ps 33:1-12	C	Sep 4-10	Ps 115:1-11	C
Jun 5-11	Ps 33:1-12	R	Sep 11-17	Ps 114	R
Jun 5-11	Ps 50:7-15	R	Sep 11-17	Ps 103:(1-7), 8-13	R
Jun 5-11	Ps 13	C			
Jun 12-18	Ps 116:1-2, 12-19	R	Sep 11-17	Ps 19:7-14	C
Jun 12-18	Ps 100	R	Sep 18-24	Ps 105:1-6, 37-45	R
Jun 12-18	Ps 46	C	Sep 18-24	Ps 145:1-8	R
Jun 19-25	Ps 86:1-10, 16-17	R	Sep 18-24	Ps 106:7-8, 19-23	C
Jun 19-25	Ps 69:7-10, (11-15), 16-18	R	Sep 25-Oct 1	Ps 78:1-4, 12-16	R
			Sep 25-Oct 1	Ps 25:1-9	R
Jun 19-25	Ps 91:1-10	C	Sep 25-Oct 1	Ps 99	C

James Taylor

Day	Psalm	Lect.	Day	Psalm	Lect.
Oct 2-8	Ps 19	R	Epiphany	Ps 72:1-7, 10-14	R
Oct 2-8	Ps 80:7-15	R	Epiphany	Ps 72:1-14	C
Oct 2-8	Ps 81:1-10	C	Baptism of our Lord	Ps 29	R, C
Thanksgiving (Can.)	Ps 65	R, C	Epiphany 2	Ps 139:1-6,	
Oct 9-15	Ps 106:1-6,			13-18	R
	19-23	R	Epiphany 2	Ps 63:1-8	C
Oct 9-15	Ps 23	R	Epiphany 3	Ps 62:5-12	R, C
Oct 9-15	Ps 135:1-14	C	Epiphany 4	Ps 111	R, C
Oct 16-22	Ps 99	R	Epiphany 5	Ps 147:1-11,	
Oct 16-22	Ps 96:1-9,			20c	R
	(10-13)	R	Epiphany 5	Ps 147:1-11	C
Oct 16-22	Ps 146	C	Epiphany 6	Ps 30	R
Oct 23-29	Ps 90:1-6, 13-17	R	Epiphany 6	Ps 32	C
Oct 23-29	Ps 1	R	Epiphany 7	Ps 41	R, C
Oct 23-29	Ps 128	C	Epiphany 8	Ps 103:1-13, 22	R
All Saints/Nov 01	Ps 34:1-10, 22	R	Epiphany 8	Ps 103:1-12	C
All Saints/Nov 01	Ps 34:1-10	C	Epiphany 9	Ps 81:1-10	R
Oct 30-Nov 5	Ps 107:1-7,		Transfig. (Epiph. last)	Ps 50:1-6	R, C
	33-37	R	Ash Wednesday	Ps 51:1-17	R
Oct 30-Nov 5	Ps 43	R	Ash Wednesday	Ps 51:1-12	C
Oct 30-Nov 5	Ps 127	C	Lent 1	Ps 25:1-10	R, C
Nov 6-12	Ps 78:1-7	R	Lent 2	Ps 22:23-31	R
Nov 6-12	Ps 70	R	Lent 2	Ps 105:1-11	C
Nov 6-12	Ps 50:7-15	C	Lent 3	Ps 19	R
Nov 13-19	Ps 123	R	Lent 3	Ps 19:7-14	C
Nov 13-19	Ps 90:1-8,		Lent 4	Ps 107:1-3,	
	(9-11), 12	R		17-22	R
Nov 13-19	Ps 76	C	Lent 4	Ps 137:1-6	C
Reign of Christ	Ps 100	R	Lent 5	Ps 51:1-12	R
Reign of Christ	Ps 95:1-7a	R	Lent 5	Ps 119:9-16	R
Reign of Christ	Ps 23	C	Lent 5	Ps 51:10-17	C
Thanksgiving (USA)	Ps 65	R, C	**Passion**/Palm Sunday	Ps 31:9-16	R, C
			Passion/**Palm** Sunday	Ps 118:1-2,	
Year B				19-29	R
			Passion/**Palm** Sunday	Ps 118:19-29	C
Advent 1	Ps 80:1-7, 17-19	R	Maundy Thursday	Ps 116:1-2,	
Advent 1	Ps 80:1-7	C		12-19	R
Advent 2	Ps 85:1-2, 8-13	R	Maundy Thursday	Ps 116:12-19	C
Advent 2	Ps 85:8-13	C	Good Friday	Ps 22	R
Advent 3	Ps 126	R	Good Friday	Ps 22:1-18	C
Advent 4	Ps 89:1-4,		Easter Vigil	Ps 136:1-9,	
	19-26	R, C		23-26	R
Christmas Eve/Day	Ps 96	R, C	Easter Vigil	Ps 16	R, C
Christmas Eve/Day	Ps 97	R, C	Easter Vigil	Ps 19	R, C
Christmas Eve/Day	Ps 98	R, C	Easter Vigil	Ps 30	C
1st after Christmas	Ps 148	R	Easter Vigil	Ps 33	C
1st after Christmas	Ps 111	C	Easter Vigil	Ps 42	R, C
New Year	Ps 8	R, C	Easter Vigil	Ps 43	R
Holy Name	Ps 65	C	Easter Vigil	Ps 46	R, C
2nd after Christmas	Ps 147:12-20	R, C	Easter Vigil	Ps 98	R, C

Everyday Psalms   189

Day	Psalm	Lect.	Day	Psalm	Lect.
Easter Vigil	Ps 143	R, C	Aug 7-13	Ps 130	R
Easter Vigil	Ps 114	R, C	Aug 7-13	Ps 34:1-8	R
Easter	Ps 118:1-2, 14-24	R	Aug 7-13	Ps 143:1-8	C
Easter	Ps 118:14-24	C	Aug 14-20	Ps 111	R
Easter 2	Ps 133	R, C	Aug 14-20	Ps 34:9-14	R
Easter 3	Ps 4	R, C	Aug 14-20	Ps 102:1-12	C
Easter 4	Ps 23	R, C	Aug 21-27	Ps 84	R
Easter 5	Ps 22:25-31	R, C	Aug 21-27	Ps 34:15-22	R
Easter 6	Ps 98	R, C	Aug 21-27	Ps 67	C
Ascension	Ps 47	R, C	Aug 28-Sep 3	Ps 45:1-2, 6-9	R
Ascension	Ps 93	R	Aug 28-Sep 3	Ps 15	R
Easter 7	Ps 1	R, C	Aug 28-Sep 3	Ps 121	C
Pentecost	Ps 104:24-34, 35b	R	Sep 4-10	Ps 125	R
			Sep 4-10	Ps 146	R
Pentecost	Ps 104:24-34	C	Sep 4-10	Ps 119:129-136	C
Trinity Sunday	Ps 29	R, C	Sep 11-17	Ps 19	R
May 29-Jun 4	Ps 139:1-6, 13-18	R	Sep 11-17	Ps 116:1-9	R
			Sep 11-17	Ps 125	C
May 29-Jun 4	Ps 81:1-10	R	Sep 18-24	Ps 1	R
May 29-Jun 4	Ps 20	C	Sep 18-24	Ps 54	R
Jun 5-11	Ps 138	R	Sep 18-24	Ps 27:1-6	C
Jun 5-11	Ps 130	R	Sep 25-Oct 1	Ps 124	R
Jun 5-11	Ps 57	C	Sep 25-Oct 1	Ps 19:7-14	R
Jun 12-18	Ps 20	R	Sep 25-Oct 1	Ps 27:7-14	C
Jun 12-18	Ps 92:1-4, 12-15	R	Oct 2-8	Ps 26	R
Jun 12-18	Ps 46	C	Oct 2-8	Ps 8	R
Jun 19-25	Ps 9:9-20	R	Oct 2-8	Ps 128	C
Jun 19-25	Ps 133	R	Thanksgiving (Can.)	Ps 126	R, C
Jun 19-25	Ps 107:1-3, 23-32	R	Oct 9-15	Ps 22:1-15	R
			Oct 9-15	Ps 90:12-17	R
Jun 19-25	Ps 48	C	Oct 9-15	Ps 90:1-12	C
Jun 26-Jul 2	Ps 130	R	Oct 16-22	Ps 104:1-9, 24, 35c	R
Jun 26-Jul 2	Ps 30	R			
Jun 26-Jul 2	Ps 24	C	Oct 16-22	Ps 91:9-16	R
Jul 3-9	Ps 48	R	Oct 16-22	Ps 35:17-28	C
Jul 3-9	Ps 123	R	Oct 23-29	Ps 34:1-8, (19-22)	R
Jul 3-9	Ps 89:20-37	C			
Jul 10-16	Ps 24	R	Oct 23-29	Ps 126	R, C
Jul 10-16	Ps 85:8-13	R	All Saints/Nov 01	Ps 24	R
Jul 10-16	Ps 132:11-18	C	All Saints/Nov 01	Ps 24:1-6	C
Jul 17-23	Ps 89:20-37	R	Oct 30-Nov 5	Ps 146	R
Jul 17-23	Ps 23	R	Oct 30-Nov 5	Ps 119:1-8	R
Jul 17-23	Ps 53	C	Oct 30-Nov 5	Ps 119:33-48	C
Jul 24-30	Ps 14	R	Nov 6-12	Ps 127	R
Jul 24-30	Ps 145:10-18	R	Nov 6-12	Ps 146	R, C
Jul 24-30	Ps 32	C	Nov 13-19	Ps 16	R
Jul 31-Aug 6	Ps 51:1-12	R	Nov 13-19	Ps 145:8-13	C
Jul 31-Aug 6	Ps 78:23-29	R	Reign of Christ	Ps 132:1-12, (13-18)	R
Jul 31-Aug 6	Ps 34:11-22	C	Reign of Christ	Ps 93	R, C

James Taylor

Day	Psalm	Lect.	Day	Psalm	Lect.
Thanksgiving (USA)	Ps 126	R, C	Good Friday	Ps 22:1-18	C
			Easter Vigil	Ps 136:1-9, 23-26	R
Year C			Easter Vigil	Ps 16	R, C
Advent 1	Ps 25:1-10	R, C	Easter Vigil	Ps 19	R, C
Advent 2	Ps 126	C	Easter Vigil	Ps 30	C
Advent 4	Ps 80:1-7	R, C	Easter Vigil	Ps 33	C
Christmas Eve/Day	Ps 96	R, C	Easter Vigil	Ps 42	R, C
Christmas Eve/Day	Ps 97	R, C	Easter Vigil	Ps 43	R
Christmas Eve/Day	Ps 98	R, C	Easter Vigil	Ps 46	R, C
1st after Christmas	Ps 148	R	Easter Vigil	Ps 143	R, C
1st after Christmas	Ps 111	C	Easter Vigil	Ps 98	R, C
2nd after Christmas	Ps 147:12-20	R, C	Easter Vigil	Ps 114	R, C
New Year/Holy Name	Ps 8	R	Easter	Ps 118:1-2, 14-24	R
New Year	Ps 117	C	Easter	Ps 118:14-24	C
Holy Name	Ps 67	C	Easter 2	Ps 118:14-29	R
Epiphany	Ps 72:1-7, 10-14	R	Easter 2	Ps 150	R
Epiphany	Ps 72:1-14	C	Easter 2	Ps 2	C
Baptism of our Lord	Ps 29	R, C	Easter 3	Ps 30	R
Epiphany 2	Ps 36:5-10	R, C	Easter 3	Ps 30:4-12	C
Epiphany 3	Ps 19	R	Easter 4	Ps 23	R, C
Epiphany 3	Ps 19:7-14	C	Easter 5	Ps 148	R
Epiphany 4	Ps 71:1-6	R, C	Easter 5	Ps 145:13b-21	C
Epiphany 5	Ps 138	R, C	Easter 6	Ps 67	R, C
Epiphany 6	Ps 1	R, C	Ascension	Ps 47	R, C
Epiphany 7	Ps 37:1-11, 39-40	R	Ascension	Ps 110	R
Epiphany 7	Ps 37:1-11	C	Easter 7	Ps 97	R, C
Epiphany 8	Ps 92:1-4, 12-15	R, C	Pentecost	Ps 104:24-34, 35b	R
Epiphany 9	Ps 96:1-9	R	Pentecost	Ps 104:24-34	C
Transfig. (Epiph. last)	Ps 99	R, C	Trinity Sunday	Ps 8	R, C
Ash Wednesday	Ps 51:1-17	R	May 29-Jun 4	Ps 96	R
Ash Wednesday	Ps 51:1-12	C	May 29-Jun 4	Ps 96:1-9	R
Lent 1	Ps 91:1-2, 9-16	R	May 29-Jun 4	Ps 100	C
Lent 1	Ps 91:9-16	C	Jun 5-11	Ps 146	R
Lent 2	Ps 27	R	Jun 5-11	Ps 30	R
Lent 2	Ps 127	C	Jun 5-11	Ps 113	C
Lent 3	Ps 63:1-8	R	Jun 12-18	Ps 5:1-8	R
Lent 3	Ps 103:1-13	C	Jun 12-18	Ps 32	R
Lent 4	Ps 32	R	Jun 12-18	Ps 42	C
Lent 4	Ps 34:1-8	C	Jun 19-25	Ps 42 and 43	R
Lent 5	Ps 126	R, C	Jun 19-25	Ps 22:19-28	R
Passion/Palm Sunday	Ps 31:9-16	R, C	Jun 19-25	Ps 43	C
Passion/**Palm** Sunday	Ps 118:1-2, 19-29	R	Jun 26-Jul 2	Ps 77:1-2, 11-20	R
Passion/**Palm** Sunday	Ps 118:19-29	C	Jun 26-Jul 2	Ps 16	R
Maundy Thursday	Ps 116:1-2, 12-19	R	Jun 26-Jul 2	Ps 44:1-8	C
Maundy Thursday	Ps 116:12-19	C	Jul 3-9	Ps 30	R
Good Friday	Ps 22	R	Jul 3-9	Ps 66:1-9	R
			Jul 3-9	Ps 5:1-8	C
			Jul 10-16	Ps 82	R

Day	Psalm	Lect.	Day	Psalm	Lect.
Jul 10-16	Ps 25:1-10	R	Oct 30-Nov 5	Ps 119:137-144	R
Jul 10-16	Ps 139:1-12	C	Oct 30-Nov 5	Ps 32:1-7	R
Jul 17-23	Ps 52	R	Oct 30-Nov 5	Ps 65:1-8	C
Jul 17-23	Ps 15	R	Nov 6-12	Ps 145:1-5,	
Jul 17-23	Ps 139:13-18	C		17-21	R
Jul 24-30	Ps 85	R	Nov 6-12	Ps 98	R
Jul 24-30	Ps 138	R	Nov 6-12	Ps 17:1-9	R
Jul 24-30	Ps 21:1-7	C	Nov 6-12	Ps 9:11-20	C
Jul 31-Aug 6	Ps 107:1-9, 43	R	Nov 13-19	Ps 98	R
Jul 31-Aug 6	Ps 49:1-12	R	Nov 13-19	Ps 82	C
Jul 31-Aug 6	Ps 28	C	Reign of Christ		
Aug 7-13	Ps 50:1-8, 22-23	R	Nov 20-26	Ps 46	R
Aug 7-13	Ps 33:12-22	R	Reign of Christ		
Aug 7-13	Ps 14	C	Nov 20-26	Ps 95	C
Aug 14-20	Ps 80:1-2, 8-19	R	Thanksgiving (USA)	Ps 100	R, C
Aug 14-20	Ps 82	R			
Aug 14-20	Ps 10:12-18	C			
Aug 21-27	Ps 71:1-6	R			
Aug 21-27	Ps 103:1-8	R			
Aug 21-27	Ps 84	C			
Aug 28-Sep 3	Ps 81:1, 10-16	R			
Aug 28-Sep 3	Ps 112	R			
Aug 28-Sep 3	Ps 15	C			
Sep 4-10	Ps 139:1-6,				
	13-18	R			
Sep 4-10	Ps 1	R			
Sep 4-10	Ps 94:12-22	C			
Sep 11-17	Ps 14	R			
Sep 11-17	Ps 51:1-10	R			
Sep 11-17	Ps 77:11-20	C			
Sep 18-24	Ps 79:1-9	R			
Sep 18-24	Ps 113	R			
Sep 18-24	Ps 107:1-9	C			
Sep 25-Oct 1	Ps 91:1-6, 14-16	R			
Sep 25-Oct 1	Ps 146	R			
Sep 25-Oct 1	Ps 107:1, 33-43	C			
Oct 2-8	Ps 137	R			
Oct 2-8	Ps 37:1-9	R			
Oct 2-8	Ps 101	C			
Thanksgiving (Can.)	Ps 100	R, C			
Oct 9-15	Ps 66:1-12	R			
Oct 9-15	Ps 111	R			
Oct 9-15	Ps 26	C			
Oct 16-22	Ps 119:97-104	R			
Oct 16-22	Ps 121	R			
Oct 16-22	Ps 119:137-144	C			
Oct 23-29	Ps 65	R			
Oct 23-29	Ps 84:1-7	R			
Oct 23-29	Ps 3	C			
All Saints/Nov 01	Ps 149	R, C			

Notes:

1. *R = Revised Common Lectionary,
   *C = Common Lectionary
2. Rather than give "Propers" or "Sundays After Pentecost"—which always seems confusing, no matter what system one uses—I have simply given the dates of the week during which these Sundays fall.